TRICKS & TIPS

A collection of helpful programs and routines

By Joachim Sgonina
and Adrian Warner

A Data Becker Book

Published by

Abacus ▦ **Software**

Table of Contents

INTRODUCTION

INTRODUCTION

Chapter 0: Introduction

The success of Turbo Pascal is a remarkable phenomenon. Well over 400,000 copies of Turbo have been sold since its first release in 1983. This makes it one of the most popular programming languages available for the personal computer owner.

Why are so many people buying Turbo?

First, Turbo offers many fine features:

* it has a very versatile "shell" that makes it easy to use
* it is a fast development system
* it is a close implementation of the well-known Jensen and Wirth standard
* it is very reasonably priced

Second, many people are anxious to learn to program in a language other than BASIC. Most PC owners have already learned to program in BASIC. The Pascal language has earned so much respect as a "good" second language to learn and Turbo Pascal has been able to fill the bill as *the* product for these owners.

Third, professionals are always searching for ways to develop software more quickly. Turbo Pascal's features are well-suited for program development.

Enough said about the success of Turbo Pascal. You probably already own Turbo. That's why you're reading this book.

Turbo Pascal Tricks & Tips is a collection of tools and techniques to help you develop programs using Turbo Pascal more quickly. Not only does it show you how to write the Turbo source code, it shows you why. So you'll be learning programming techniques as well.

We've assumed that you're already familiar with Turbo Pascal and how to use it. You should already know how to edit a source program, set compiler options and compile the program into an executable program. We're not going to teach you how to do these things. That is better left to tutorials on Turbo Pascal. But we will teach you techniques.

The best way to use **Tricks & Tips** is to sit down at your computer with the book and start entering the programs. After you have the programs running correctly, you shouldn't be afraid to experiment by adding your own code for features that meet your particular needs and requirements. We're very anxious to hear back from you on how you're using the techniques explained here.

We certainly hope that you learn a lot from these tricks and tips.

CHAPTER 1

Chapter 1: Sorting

Modern data processing systems help people manage large quantities of data quickly and effectively--in business and government, the arts and sciences and almost every area of modern life. Taking inventory in a warehouse, preparing the factory payroll and analyzing monthly sales performance are but a few of the more common applications.

In all of these applications, *sorting* is one of the most fundamental procedures used in data processing. Sorting helps to manage data in existing systems as well as the new data being entered daily. The data is sorted according to certain criteria so that a given item can be found more quickly, either by the computer itself or a user of the system.

In this chapter we'll discuss in detail the topic of sorting data. We'll present several methods of sorting (algorithms) and show how they help solve data-sorting problems.

In commercial applications, sorting data often uses more than 20% of the available computing time. For this reason, sorting is quite important. Today, every commercial data management software package contains a sorting function and the efficiency of this function often determines the overall effectiveness and success of the software package.

Sorting is defined as a procedure which places a set of objects (numbers, characters, words, etc.) into a specific order according to classes or sorts. In this chapter, we'll make this definition more specific: objects are sorted according to their value (such as the alphabetical order of last names in a telephone book). A set of objects sorted in this manner is indicated by the linear ordering of its elements. This is why presorted lists can be searched much more efficiently than unsorted lists.

We'll distinguish between two different types of sorting procedures that depend on the structure of the data to be sorted.

To the first group belong sorting algorithms which sort the data in main memory (internal sort). Thanks to the fast access time of memory, there are very efficient sorting algorithms if the data can be sorted in memory. But since the amount of main memory is relatively small compared to the amount of data to be processed, these sorting algorithms have limited use.

The second group is comprised of procedures that sort data in sequential files. In contrast to the first group, these sort algorithms are significantly slower because of this sequential access to disk files.

When comparing the efficiency of a sorting procedure, we must consider two factors: execution time and space requirements. The execution time of a sorting procedure is equal to the time required to sort n number of data records. The two most important variables determining the execution time are:

Q = number of exchange or move operations
C = number of comparison operations

The space requirement is the amount of memory required by the records to be sorted and any temporary space.

In commercial data processing, the objects to be sorted consist of a key (number, name, etc.) and information associated with that key. An object might have the following structure:

```
type Object= record
             ident: integer;
           end;
```

For the sorting procedure, `ident` is the key component by which the data is to be ordered. To keep things simple, `integer` is used for the type of the key component, although it could just as easily be `char` or `string`.

1.1 Sorting in memory

Sorting data in internal memory is especially important in systems programs and compilers, since these programs require effective use of the scarce memory space. There are a number of very different sorting algorithms available to the programmer. Each of these procedures is tailored for specific requirements, such as model of computer, length of the list to be sorted or the type of data.

For internal sorting, objects are usually in an arrary of in the form of a linked list. In the following sections we'll present procedures that sort objects in an array according to their value. The objects can have the same structure as the previous data type `Object`, for example. In this section, the sort algorithms will process an array of the following form:

```
type Arr = array[1..n] of Object;
```

Basically, sorting algorithms which work on data in internal memory can be divided into three groups: sorting by selection, by insertion and by exchange. Each of these procedures characterizes a specific method of sorting which can be improved and optimized according to the application.

1.1.1 Sorting by selection

First we'll take a look at the simplest procedure - sorting by selection.

Consider an array of n elements. The goal is to arrange the elements so that the element with the smallest value is at beginning of the array and the element with the largest value is at the end of the array. The sorting procedure consists of two steps: selecting the array element (from among n elements) with the largest value and exchanging it with the last element in the array (unless this last element already has the largest value).

This procedure is then repeated. But now you need only select the largest array element from among the first $n-1$ array elements. Remember, we've already placed the element with the largest value in the last (nth) array position. So now we're selecting the element with the next largest value. Then we can exchange it with the second to last element in the array (the $n-1$st element).

When the procedure is repeated the third time, only the first $n-2$ elements need be searched. And at the conclusion, the $n-2$nd element will have the third largest value. Each time the array is searched, the sorting procedure is said to have made a *pass*. Thus, sorting by selection requires at least $n-1$ passes through the array.

The following example illustrates sorting by selection by showing you the order of the array at the conclusion of the individual passes:

	start of array				end of array	
array to be sorted:	61	15	84	10	51	7
first pass	61	15	7	10	51	84
second pass	51	15	7	10	61	84
third pass	10	15	7	51	61	84
fourth pass	10	7	15	51	61	84
fifth pass	7	10	15	51	61	84

Procedure `SelectSort` is an implementation of this sorting procedure. This procedure uses the previously defined types `Arr` and `Object`.

```pascal
procedure SelectSort(var x:Arr;n:integer);

var temp,index,k,n:integer;
    swap:Object;

begin
  for index:=n downto 2 do
    begin
      k:=index;
      temp:=x[1].ident;
      for m:=1 to index do
        if temp<=x[m].ident then
          begin
            temp:=x[m].ident
            k:=m
          end;
      swap:=x[k];
      x[k]:=x[index];
      x[index]:=swap;
    end
end;
```

`SelectSort` operates on the array of type `Arr` passed through reference parameter `x`. The value parameter `n` passes the number of elements in the array to be sorted.

This first sorting procedure is the simplest but also the slowest. The number of comparisons in the **for**-loop `index` is `index-1`. The number of comparison can be calculated as follows:

$$C = (n^2 - n) / 2$$
where n = number of elements to be sorted

In this procedure, at least $3*(n-1)$ exchanges are performed.

A significant improvement to this procedure was made by J. William in 1964. His algorithm known as the *heap sort.* derives better performance by requiring fewer comparisons. In contrast to the previous example, the information obtained through each comparison is used to construct a selection-binary tree from the array.

In an array of n elements, the first element is declared the *root* of the tree. Each element of the array is at the same time a *node* of the binary tree, and can be assigned a left and a right branch. This assignment can be represented with the following formula:

left descendent of `i` = $2*i$
right descendent of `i` = $2*i+1$

(i, $2*i$, and $2*i+1$ must be less than or equal to n)

An array with ten elements can be illustrated with the following binary tree:

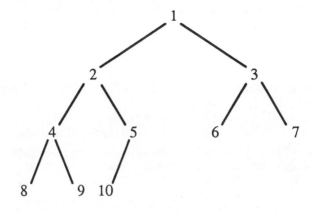

Based on this structure, a heap can now be built. An array is called a heap if the following applies for all n elements:

* the value of the `i`th array element is greater than or equal to the value of the `2*i`th and the `2*i+1`st array element

  (`i, 2*i, 2*i+1` are less than or equal to n)

This condition forces a binary tree, in which the value of the *parent* is greater than or equal to the left and right children.

If we choose an eight-element array with the values 76, 13, 27, 55, 91, 39, 1 and 48 as an example, the corresponding heap looks like this:

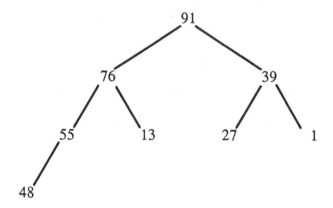

The largest element of a heap is always the first element in the array. Such a heap is also called a maximal heap. A minimal heap can be defined similarly. A minimal heap must also adhere to the rule that the parent cannot be larger than its left or right child.

The heap-sort procedure can be roughly divided into two steps:

1. The array is transformed into a heap.

2. The first (smallest or largest) element is exchanged with the last (largest or smallest) element of the array and the array is shortened by the last element.

If these steps are repeated n−1 times, we have a sorted array. The array is shortened by one element after each step.

The operation of this algorithm can be seen in the following example:

	start of array						end of array	
array to be sorted:	76	13	27	55	91	39	1	48
First pass	76	55	39	48	13	27	1	91
Second pass	55	48	39	1	13	27	76	91
Third pass	48	27	39	1	13	55	76	91
Fourth pass	39	27	13	1	48	55	76	91
Fifth pass	27	1	13	39	48	55	76	91
Sixth pass	13	1	27	39	48	55	76	91
Seventh pass	1	13	27	39	48	55	76	91

In the first pass, the array is converted to a heap by using two partial transformations. Then the first element of the current array is exchanged with the last.

Initial tree:

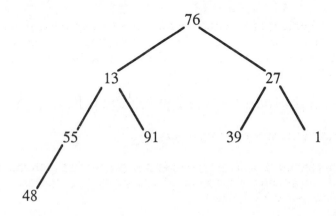

is transformed to:

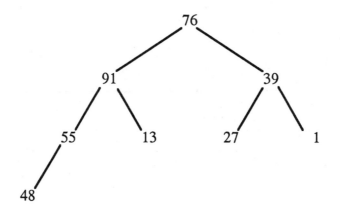

and transformed again to:

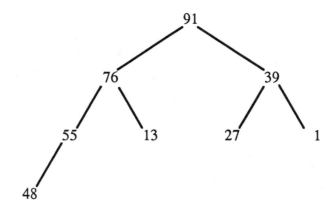

Now that the heap is constructed, the first element of the current array can be exchanged with the last. The exchanged elements are no longer shown in the illustration.

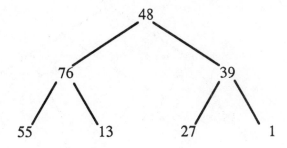

is transformed to:

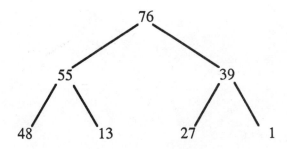

Exchange:

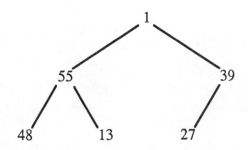

is transformed to:

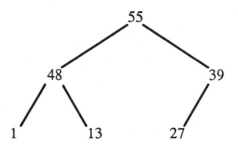

Exchange:

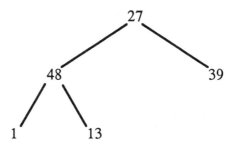

is transformed to:

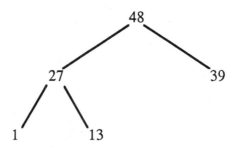

Exchange:

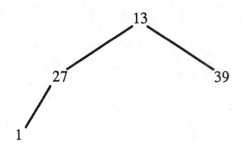

is transformed to:

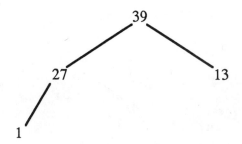

Exchange:

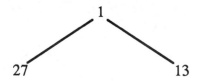

is transformed to:

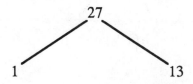

Exchange:

13

1

Exchange:

1

The procedure is then finished and the array is sorted.

The following procedure, Heap, is an implementation of this method:

```pascal
procedure Heap(var x:Arr;n:integer);
var left,right,index,j:integer;
    temp:Object;
    ok:boolean;
begin
  left:=(n div 2)+1
  right:=n;
  while right>=2 do
    begin
      if left<2 then
        begin
          temp:=x[1];
          x[1]:=x[right];
          x[right]:=temp;
          index:=1;
          right:=right-1;
        end
      else
        begin
          left:=left-1;
          index:=left
        end;
      temp:=x[index];
```

```
      ok:=false;
      j:=2*index;
      while not(ok) and (right>=j) do
        begin
          if j<right then
            if x[j].ident<x[j+1].ident then j:=j+1;
          if temp.ident >= x[j].ident then
            ok:=true
          else
            begin
              x[index]:=x[j];
              index:=j;
              j:=2*index
            end;
        end;
    x[index]:=temp
  end;
end;
```

The algorithm uses the familiar data types `Object` and `Arr`. The local variable `right` contains the length of the current array; and the value of the variable `left` is changed relative to this quantity.

The variable `left` indicates the last parent node; that is, all nodes with a greater index are *leaves* of the tree. The first **if** statement determines if the next operation is exchange or balance. The following **while**-loop transforms the array into a heap.

The execution time of the heap sort is very efficient $(n*ld(n))$. In contrast to the previous procedure, the execution time of the heap sort does not vary much even in the most extreme cases.

1.1.2 Sorting by insertion

In this section we present a new sort procedure based on the principle of insertion. Almost everyone has used this procedure when putting their playing card hand in order.

In this procedure, the elements are sorted without the need for an additional array. To begin, the first two elements of the array are compared and placed into the proper order based on their values. Next, the third element of the array is placed into the partial list consisting of the first two elements based on its value. In the next step, the fourth array element is placed in its proper position in this three-element partial list. The method is repeated using the fifth, sixth, etc. elements. The insertion point in the partial list is determined by comparing the element to be sorted with the elements already in the partial list.

Here's an example:

sequence to be sorted	58	9	81	25	73	13	64	31
First pass		9	58	81	25	73	13	64	31
Second pass		9	58	81	25	73	13	64	31
Third pass		9	25	58	81	73	13	64	31
Fourth pass		9	25	58	73	81	13	64	31
Fifth pass		9	13	25	58	73	81	64	31
Sixth pass		9	13	25	58	64	73	81	31
Seventh pass		9	13	25	31	58	64	73	81

The following procedure Insertion uses this method:

```
procedure Insertion(var x:Arr;n:integer);

var index,j:integer;
    temp:Object;
    ok:boolean;

begin
  for index:=2 to n do
    begin
      temp:=x[index];
      j:=index-1;
      ok:=true;
      while (x[j].ident > temp.ident) and ok do
        begin
```

```
          x[j+1]:=x[j];
          j:=j-1;
          if j <= 0 then ok:=false
        end;
      x[j+1]:=temp
    end;
end;
```

Inserting an element in the partial list is a time-consuming process. This procedure requires an average of $j/2$ comparisons (j is equal to the length of the partial list). Since the **for**-loop is executed $n-1$ times, an average of $(n^2 - n)/4$ comparisons are performed. The number of exchanges on average for the whole algorithm is about $(n^2 + n)/4$.

The unfavorable execution time of this procedure can be improved by reducing the number of comparisons. These can be substantially reduced by making use of the linear order of the partial list and by using a *binary search* for the insertion point instead of the sequential search used in the above Pascal procedure.

A binary search is based on cutting the partial list (which is already ordered) in half until the insertion point is found. The following procedure B_Insertion is one implementation of this modified algorithm:

```
procedure B_Insertion(var x:Arr;n:integer);

var index,right,left,i,j:integer;
    temp:Object;

begin
  for index:=2 to n do
    begin
      temp:=x[index];
      right:=index-1;
      left:=1;
      repeat
        j:=(left + right) div 2;
        if x[j].ident > temp.ident then
          right:=j-1
        else
          left:=j+1;
      until left > right;
```

```
    for i:=index-1 downto left do
        x[i+1]:=x[i];
      x[left]:=temp
    end
end;
```

Using this procedure, the average number of comparisons is reduced to `n*ld(n)`. Unfortunately, this has no effect on the number of exchange operations required.

Sorting by insertion, however, can be made more efficient by performing the exchange operations over longer distances. This is the principle D.L. Shell used in the sorting algorithm he presented in 1959.

In this procedure, the array to be sorted is divided into `array_length` (number of elements) `div 2` partial lists in the first pass, whereby the distance of the elements in the partial lists from each other is `array_length div 2`. All partial lists are then sorted one after the other. In the second pass, the distance between the elements of a partial list is halved; the length of the partial lists then double automatically. These new partial lists are then sorted. This procedure is repeated in the next pass. In the last pass the distance between the elements of a sequence is one, which means that there is only one partial list, whose length corresponds to the `array_length`.

At first glance this procedure seems very time-consuming, but its execution time is better than the simple insertion method. In the last pass of the Shell algorithm the list is already well-ordered and needs only a few exchange operations.

In the following example this procedure can be seen used on an array of with eight elements:

sequence to be sorted: 10 49 90 31   9 75 82 26

First pass   Partial lists (10,9) (49,75) (90,82) (31,26)
                    9 49 82 26 10 75 90 31

Second pass   Partial lists (9,82,10,90) (49,26,75,31)
                    9 26 10 31 82 49 90 75

Third pass   Partial lists (9,26,10,31,82,49,90,75)
                    9 10 26 31 49 75 82 90

The procedure Shell is an implementation of this method in Turbo Pascal:

```
procedure Shell(var x:Arr;n;integer);

var index,phase,distance,l,pot,i,j:integer;
    temp:Object;

begin
  phase:=(n div 2) * 2 div 2 -1;
  for i:=phase downto 1 do
    begin
      pot:=1;
      for l:=1 to 1-1 do pot:=pot*2;
      distance:=pot;
      for j:=distance+1 to n do
        begin
          temp:=x[j];
          index:=j-distance;
          while (x[index].ident > temp.ident) and
                (index>0) do
            begin
              x[index+distance]:=x[index];
              index:=index - distance
            end;
          x[index+distance]:=temp;
        end;
    end;
end;
```

The number of passes required is determined in the first line of the program. The first inner **for**-loop calculates the current distance of the elements of a partial list; the second sorts each of the lists. The **while**-loop sorts the partial lists themselves.

The average execution time of this procedure is $n*n^{1/2}$.

1.1.3 Sorting by exchange

Now we'll present some sorting algorithms that are based on the principle of direct exchange of the array elements. The first procedure compares neighboring elements and exchanges them based on the result of the comparison. The other procedures differ mainly in the method used for the exchanges.

The *bubble sort* method is based on a simple but relatively time-consuming method. An array is processed from from beginning to end by exchanging neighboring elements if the first element is greater than the second element. In this manner, the largest element "bubbles up" to the end of the array. In the next pass, the procedure is applied to one less element of the array, because the largest element in the entire array is already in the end position. At the end of each pass, the largest elements of the array are always at the extreme end. The procedure is terminated when the remaining array has only one element.

If you picture the array as standing vertically, the rising elements of the array can be compared to an air bubble; hence the name.

The individual steps of this procedure can be seen in the following example (elements are left to right instead of top to bottom):

sequence to be sorted:	23	56	89	12	34	45	67	3
First pass	23	56	12	34	45	67	3	89
Second pass	23	12	34	45	56	3	67	89
Third pass	12	23	34	45	3	56	67	89
Fourth pass	12	23	34	3	45	56	67	89
Fifth pass	12	23	3	34	45	56	67	89
Sixth pass	12	3	23	34	45	56	67	89
Seventh pass	3	12	23	34	45	56	67	89

The procedure Bubble is an implementation of this process:

```
procedure Bubble(var x:Arr;n:integer);

var index,i:integer;
    temp:Object;

begin
  for i:=n downto 2 do
    begin
      for index:=2 to i+1 do
        if x[index-1].ident > x[index].ident then
          begin
            temp:=x[index-1];
            x[index-1]:=x[index];
            x[index]:=temp
          end;
    end;
end;
```

The inner **for**-loop makes the passes through the remaining elements of the array with the implicit comparisons and appropriate exchanges. The outer **for**-loop continually reduces the number of remaining elements.

This procedure requires an average of $(n^2-n)/4$ exchanges and $(n^2-n)/2$ comparisons. The bubble sort can be improved slightly with the addition of a routine which detects an already sorted sequence. This addition does not have a substantial reduction in the execution time. The sort procedure presented above can be made more efficient by constantly changing the direction of the passes.

In contrast to the bubble sort, in which the remaining elements are always processed from beginning to end seeking the largest element, the Shaker procedure works this way: the remaining elements are first searched from top to bottom for the smallest element, and this is placed at the start of the array. The number of remaining elements is then reduced by one. The top to bottom search for the largest element is then made. This element is placed at the end of the remaining elements and the number is reduced by one. During the course of this procedure the number of elements to be sorted converges to zero; once the number reaches one, the sort algorithm is ended.

You can follow the individual phases of this sort procedure in the following representation:

```
                start of array              end of array
                     |                           |
sequence to be sorted:  59 13 95 48 72   8   2  47

First pass              2 59 13 95 48 72   8  47

Second pass             2 13 59 48 72   8  47  95

Third pass              2   8 13 59 48 72  47  95

Fourth pass             2   8 13 48 59 47  72  95

Fifth pass              2   8 13 47 48 59  72  95

Sixth pass              2   8 13 47 48 59  72  95
```

The procedure Shaker is an implementation of this process:

```
procedure Shaker(var x:Arr;n:integer);

var index,i,j,left,right:integer;
    temp:Object;

begin
  left:=2;
  right:=n;
  index:=n;
  while left <= right do
    begin
      for i:=right downto left do
        if x[i-1].ident > x[i].ident then
          begin
            temp:=x[i-1];
            x[i-1]:=x[i];
            x[i]:=temp;
            index:=i
          end;
        left:=index+1;
        for j:=left to right do
          if x[j-1].ident > x[j].ident then
            begin
              temp:=x[j-1];
```

```
                x[j-1]:=x[j];
                x[j]:=temp;
                index:=j
             end;
          right:=index-1
     end;
end;
```

The **while**-loop is executed until the left boundary (`left`) crosses the right boundary (`right`) of the array left to be sorted. With each execution of the **while**-loop, the smallest element is found with the help of the first **for**-loop and placed at the start. The second **for**-loop repeats the procedure in the opposite direction. The execution time of this improved bubble sort is slightly better than that of its predecessor because of the lower number of comparisons.

The *quick-sort* procedure is the fastest algorithm in this class of sorts. It was introduced in 1962 by C.A.R. Hoare, and is based on the fact that exchanges are efficient only when they are made over long distances in the array. The algorithm presented by Hoare divides the entire array into several small arrays which are processed recursively and then combined into a sorted array.

An arbitrary element is selected from the unsorted array and assigned to a variable such as `temp`. Comparisons and exchanges of the array elements are made with the variable `temp`. The goal is that all larger elements will be on the right of `temp` and all smaller elements will be on the left. The procedure is then reapplied to each of the two partial arrays. This division is continued until the partial arrays have a length of one. The entire array is then sorted.

The quick-sort procedure makes the following passes:

```
sequence to be sorted:  85 42 97 23 35 28  3 14

First pass              14  3 23 97 35 28 42 85

Second pass              3 14 23 97 35 28 42 85

Third pass               3 14 23 97 35 28 42 85

Fourth pass              3 14 23 28 35 97 42 85
```

```
Fifth pass          3 14 23 28 35 97 42 85

Sixth pass          3 14 23 28 35 85 42 97

Seventh pass        3 14 23 28 35 42 85 97

Eigth pass          3 14 23 28 35 42 85 97

Ninth pass          3 14 23 28 35 42 85 97
```

The procedure Quick presents this procedure:

```
procedure Quick(var x:Arr,n:integer);

procedure Sort(left,right:integer);

var i,j:integer;
    temp1,temp2:Object;

begin
  i:=left;
  j:=right;
  temp1:=x[(i+j) div 2];
  while i < j do
    begin
      while x[j].ident < temp1.ident do i:=i+1;
      while x[j].ident > temp1.ident do j:=j-1;
      if i <= j then
        begin
          temp2:=x[i];
          x[i]:=x[j];
          x[j]:=temp2;
          i:=i+1;
          j:=j-1;
        end
    end;
  if left < j then sort(left,j);
  if i < right then sort(i,right)
end;

begin
  if n > 1 then sort(1,n)
end;
```

The inner procedure Sort is called specifying the array boundaries only once. It processes the array until it is sorted. The current partial array boundaries are given in variables i and j at the start of the Sort procedure. The index of the arbitrary array element results from the expression (left + right) div 2. The variables i and j are implicit pointers which are moved towards the comparison element temp1 in the two inner **while**-loops until they encounter a larger or smaller element. In this case, the two elements are exchanged. The outer **while**-loop allows this to continue until both pointers encounter each other. If this loop is processed as well, the left and then the right partial array can be sorted through the recursive call of the Sort procedure.

The average number of comparisons required in this sort algorithm is n*ln(n). The average number of exchanges is equal to the number of comparisons. Empirical studies have shown that the quick sort is superior to all other methods of sorting. This procedure is well suited for sorting large arrays, but its execution time is not as favorable for smaller arrays.

1.2 Sorting Files

Up to now we have presented sorting procedures which are suited for sorting arrays in memory. In commercial applications, it's often the case that sets of data must be managed which are many times too large to fit into main memory and must be stored on external storage media (files). In the following section we'll introduce several sorting methods for files which work on the principle of merging two partial lists.

Let's suppose that we have two presorted files that we want to combine into a single ordered file. The process is called *merging*. In this simplest case of merging, you read an element from each of the two files, compare the two, and write the smaller to a third file. The next element is read from the file which contained the smaller of the two just compared. This process is repeated until both files are empty. The third file resulting from this is then ordered and is called the merged file.

Unfortunately, this case is rare. The principle of merging can be used in a modified form to sort unordered files however. In this sort procedure, an attempt is first made to generate ordered partial lists. These partial lists are then continually lengthened through merging. The following is performed in this procedure: File A (the file to be sorted) is split into two parts containing equal number of elements. The first part is copied into file B and the second part into file C. Next, an element is read from file B and C and these elements are written as an ordered partial list of length two into file A. This merging process is repeated until all components of the two initial files B and C are in file A. The procedure continues by splitting A into two parts again. The ordered partial lists placed into B and C in the first step are read in and made into a new ordered partial list of length four and placed in file A. Again, this process is repeated until files B and C are empty. In the next pass, file A is divided again, copied into files B and C, and the ordered partial lists are merged into ordered partial lists of length eight. The passes are repeated until file A is finally sorted.

Each pass of this merge procedure can be divided into two distinct phases:

1. Splitting file A
2. Merging the ordered partial lists

This procedure can be followed in this example:

    Unsorted file A: 74 42 93 18   5 29 31 17

    First pass *********************

-Split   File B: 74 42 93 18
            File C: 5 29 31 17

-Merge   File A: 5 74/29 42/32 93/17 18

    Second pass *********************

-Split   File B: 5 74 29 42
            File C: 31 93 17 18

-Merge   File A: 5 31 74 93/17 18 29 42

    Third Pass *********************

-Split   File B: 5 31 74 93
            File C: 17 18 29 42

-Merge   File A: 5 17 18 29 31 42 74 93

    End of Sort *********************

In the last pass, two completely ordered files (partial lists) are sorted by merging.

In each pass, n exchange operations and n comparisons take place. In each new pass, the length of the ordered partial lists doubles so that after ln(n) passes the original file is completely sorted.

Unfortunately, this procedure has some disadvantages. The most time-consuming operations a computer must perform are reading and writing files. In each pass, file A must first be divided into files B and C in the first phase before the second phase (merging) can be started. The splitting can be made more efficient by using a fourth file, file D.

When merging files A and B, for example, the first half of the resulting list can be written to file C and the other half to file D. In the next pass, files C and D are merged and divided between files A and B. The first phase of each pass can be omitted except in the first pass. Another disadvantage of

27

this lies in the fact that presorted partial lists in the original file are not recognized. The "natural" partial lists can be merged with little effort in place of the "artificially" created ordered partial lists.

In the technical literature, the term *run* indicates a naturally ordered partial list. A file is sorted only when it consists of a single run. The end of a run is relatively easy to determine due to the sequential structure of the file. A run is finished when the value of the next element is less than the one preceding it. In the following example, individual runs are separated from each other by a slash.

```
14 27 55 / 76 91 / 25 58 64 88 / 10 90 / 49 / 8 66
```

As in preceeding procedure, the first half of a run is written to file B and the other half to file C in this modified merge-sort procedure, also called *natural merge*. For the sake of simplicity, one run is written to file B, the next to file C, and so on. In the next step, the runs in files B and C are merged into file C. With each new pass the number of runs is cut in half. In the last pass, there is one run in file B and one run in file C (both files are ordered) which are then combined into the sorted file A by merging.

In the natural merge procedure, the following phases are processed:

Unsorted file A: 72/24 97/ 5 29/54/33 70

First pass **********************

-Split   File B: 72/ 5 29/33 70
            File C: 24 97/54

-Merge   File A: 24 72 97/ 5 29 54/33 70

Second pass ********************

-Split   File B: 24 72 97/33 70
            File C: 5 29 54

-Merge   File A: 5 24 29 54 72 97/33 70

Third pass ***********************

-Split   File B: 5 24 29 54 72 97
              File C: 33 70

-Merge   File A: 5 24 29 33 54 70 72 97

End of sort ***********************

The natural merge procedure can also be improved in several areas. The division of runs can be made more efficient. Instead of dividing the resulting file after each merge, the runs from two source files are merged and written to the result file until one of the source files is empty. This file is then declared the new source file and the merging continues.

The greatest effectiveness of this sort procedure is reached when the number of runs in the initial file is equal to a Fibonacci number. Fibonacci numbers are defined recursively. Each Fibonnacci number is generated from the sum of its two predecessors. The first 12 numbers are:

0, 1, 1, 2, 3, 5, 8, 13, 21, 34, 55, 89, ...

In the first pass the runs of the initial file are divided between source files B and C so that the number of runs in each source file is again a Fibonacci number. For example, if we have 21 runs in the initial file, the source files would contain 13 and 8 runs, respectively. When one merges the two source files according to the method described above and places the result in file A, the sum of the runs of the result file (8) and of the remaining source file (5) is equal to the next smaller Fibonacci number (13). The following example clarifies this merge procedure:

Pass	A	B	C	Sum of runs
0	0	13	8	21
1	8	5	0	13
2	3	0	5	8
3	0	3	2	5
4	2	1	0	3
5	1	0	1	2
6	1	0	0	1

More often than not, the number of runs in the source file is not a Fibonnaci number. This disadvantage can be eliminated in a preliminary pass by decreasing the number of runs through internal sorting, for example.

The natural merge can be accelerated by an artificial increase in the length of the runs. Before the first pass is started, a procedure is activated to load the file section-by-section into an array, to sort the array using an internal sort procedure, andto write the run to the starting file. This both reduces the number of runs in the original file and increases their length.

The following program FileSort represents the implementation of this procedure:

```
program FileSort;

  type
   Object = record
     ident : integer;
     info : string[80];
    end;
   Fil = file of Object;

  var
   A, B, C : Fil;
   Run : boolean;
   RNumber, index1, index2 : integer;

  procedure PreSort;

   type
    buffer = array[1..100] of Object;

   var
    Arr : buffer;
    index1, index2, length : integer;

    procedure ReadIn (var lbound, rbound :
  integer);

     var
      m : integer;
```

```
begin
 m := 1;
 while (m <= 100) and not eof(A) do
  begin
    read(A, Arr[m]);
    m := m + 1;
  end;
 rbound := lbound + m
end;

procedure Heap (var x : buffer;
        n : integer);

 var
   left, right, index, j : integer;
   temp : Object;
   ok : boolean;

begin
 left := (n div 2) + 1;
 right := n;
 while right >= 2 do
  begin
    if left < 2 then
     begin
       temp := x[1];
       x[1] := x[right];
       x[right] := temp;
       index := 1;
       right := right - 1;
      end
    else
     begin
       left := left - 1;
       index := left;
      end;
    temp := x[index];
    ok := false;
    j := 2 * index;
    while not (ok) and (right >= j) do
     begin
       if j < right then
        if x[j].ident < x[j + 1].ident then
          j := j + 1;
```

```
      if temp.ident >= x[j].ident then
       ok := true
      else
       begin
        x[index] := x[j];
        index := j;
        j := 2 * index
       end
     end;
    x[index] := temp
   end
end;

procedure Save (lbound, rbound : integer);

 var
   j, n : integer;

begin
 n := rbound - lbound;
 seek(A, lbound - 1);
 for j := 1 to n do
  write(A, Arr[j])
end;

begin
 reset(A);
 index1 := 1;
 index2 := index1;
 repeat
  ReadIn(index1, index2);
  length := index2 - index1;
  Heap(Arr, length);
  Save(index1, index2);
  index1 := index2;
 until eof(A)
end;

procedure Copy (var x, y : Fil;
        var index : integer);

 var
   temp1, temp2 : Object;
```

```
begin
 read(x, temp1);
 index := index + 1;
 write(y, temp1);
 if eof(x) then
  Run := false
 else
  begin
   read(x, temp2);
   seek(x, index);
   if temp2.ident < temp1.ident then
    Run := false;
  end
end;

procedure CreateRun (var x, y : Fil;
        var index : integer);

begin
 Run := true;
 while Run do
  copy(x, y, index);
end;

procedure Split;

begin
 writeln;
 index1 := 0;
 index2 := 0;
 repeat
  CreateRun(A, B, index1);
  if not eof(A) then
   begin
    CreateRun(A, C, index1)
   end
 until eof(A);
end;

procedure MergeRun;

 var
  temp3, temp4 : Object;
```

```
begin
 Run := true;
 repeat
  read(B, temp3);
  seek(B, index1);
  read(C, temp4);
  seek(C, index2);
  if temp3.ident < temp4.ident then
   begin
    copy(B, A, index1);
    if not Run then
     CreateRun(C, A, index2)
   end
  else
   begin
    copy(C, A, index2);
    if not Run then
     CreateRun(B, A, index1);
   end
 until not Run
end;

procedure Merge;

begin
 index1 := 0;
 index2 := 0;
 repeat
  MergeRun;
  RNumber := RNumber + 1
 until eof(B) or eof(C);
 while not eof(B) do
  begin
   CreateRun(B, A, index1);
   RNumber := RNumber + 1
  end;
 while not eof(C) do
  begin
   CreateRun(C, A, index2);
   RNumber := RNumber + 1
  end
end;
```

```
procedure Activate;

begin
 repeat
   rewrite(B);
   rewrite(C);
   reset(A);
   Split;
   reset(B);
   reset(C);
   rewrite(A);
   RNumber := 0;
   Merge;
 until RNumber = 1
end;


begin
 assign (A,'Source.dat ');
 assign(B,'Bfile.dat');
 assign(C,'CFile.dat');
 PreSort;
 Activate;
 close(A);
 close(B);
 close(C);
 erase(B);
 erase(C)
end.
```

Procedure PreSort reads 100 objects from the file Source.dat
(local procedure ReadIn), puts them in the array Arr, sorts the array
(local procedure Heap), and writes the presorted elements into the starting
file (local procedure Save).

Procedure ReadIn recognizes an end of file before 100 records are read
in the last past and passes this information to the heap sort.

Procedure Activiate manages the two phases of the natural merge. It
calls the procedures Split and Merge until the Source.dat file is
finally sorted. The task of procedure Split is to evenly transfer the runs
from Source.dat to Bfile.dat and Cfile.dat. For this purpose,
another routine, CreateRun, is called. It organizes the copying of a run.

Procedure `Copy` serves to copy an element from one file to another. In the second phase of a pass, the procedure `Merge` is called. Here the procedure `MergeRun`, which merges two runs, is called until the end of the `Bfile.dat` or `Cfile.dat` is reached. Runs remaining in either of the two files are subsequently copied to the `Source.dat` file. The sorting procedure is done when only one run remains (`RNumber=1`). The files `Bfile.dat` and `Cfile.dat` are erased before the program ends.

CHAPTER 2

Chapter 2:   Trees

Linear lists or arrays can be represented by means of a simple graphic structure in which each component has a single sucessor(except for the last component).

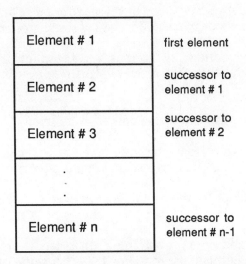

In many applications, this simple data structure is not sufficient. Other data structures can have multiple successors. Some common examples are the family tree, the corporate organization charts or a table of contents diagram.

Here's one such representation of Chapter 1 of this book as a simple structure:

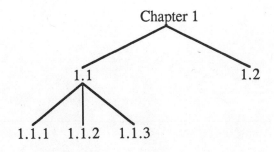

This type of structure is called a *tree*. Each element of the tree is called a node and an element without a successor is called a *leaf*. For example, element 1.1.2 in the previous diagram is a leaf. Trees are used extensively in data processing, especially when it is important to find elements in a given order as quickly as possible. Certain elements in an array can be found quite quickly. But to do this, the entire array must be in memory. Since the main memory capacity of most computers is limited, special methods and structures have been developed for these applications. Before exploring these methods, we should first lay some groundwork.

A tree can be defined in various ways, though the definitions are equivalent to each other. Here are two different definitions of the tree structure.

The first definition has three rules apply to every tree:

1.Every tree has exactly one starting point or *node*, called the *root* of the tree. (`Chapter 1` in the previous diagram is a root)

2. Every node, except for the root node, has exactly one predecessor. (The predecessor of node 1.1.2 is node 1.1)

3. A sequence of nodes `n1, n2, n3, n4, ..., nn` can be assigned to every node other than the root. For $1 \leq i \leq n$: ni is the successor of ni-1.

A tree can also be defined recursively. For each tree of basic type B:

1.It is either empty or

2.It has a designated node of basic type B (root) to which are connected a finite number of subtrees of basic type B.

In this book, trees are always represented with the root at the top and the branches below it. For example:

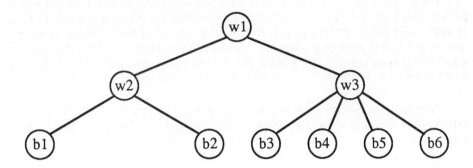

Node w1 is the root of this tree and it is connected to two subtrees. The left subtree has the node w2 as the root and the root of the right subtree is w3. In the above representation nodes b1, b2, b3, b4, b5 and b6 form the leaves of the tree. The terms *parent* and *child* are also used interchangeably with predecessor and successor. So w1 is the parent of w2 and w3, and conversely w2 and w3 are the children of w1. The same relationship applies between w2 and b1 and b2 or between w3 and b3, b4, b5 and b6.

The *order* or *degree* of a node is the largest number of its direct successors. Node w1 has two successors, node w2 also has two, and node w3 has four. The node with the greatest order also indicates the order of the entire tree. Since node w3 has the greatest order (four), the order of the whole tree is also four.

Every tree can be divided into *levels*. The root is always level zero and its direct successors are level one. The direct successors of these children have the next higher level two, and so on. The height of the tree is given by the greatest level of its elements; in our example the tree has height three.

An ordered tree is a tree with predetermined sequence of its subtrees. Each subtree of this tree must also be an ordered subtree.

2.1 Binary trees

If every node of a tree has no more than two successors (order two), it is called a binary tree. Since each node of a binary tree has a maximum of two children, they are often called the *left* child and the *right* child. In Pascal the data structure node always has two explicit pointers - one to the left and one to the right successors. Here's the data structure for a node:

```
type bintree = ^node;
     node = record
              ident : integer;
              left, right : ^bintree
            end;
```

In the following sections, the components of ident in the data structure for node is always the identifying key. Other components can be included in this record, but we've omitted them for the sake of simplicity. Any desired binary trees can be constructed with this structure.

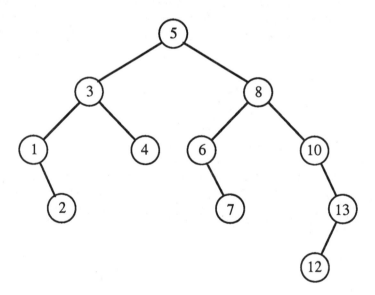

It's relatively easy to implement *operations* that work with binary trees. By operations, we mean finding nodes, adding nodes or deleting nodes from the binary trees. They can be used in most applications requiring data structures that are more complicated than simple lists or arrays.

Before we present the construction of a tree, let's talk about the term *binary search tree.*

The following applies for every binary search tree of basic type B:

1. It is either empty or

2. It has a designated node of basic type B (root) to which are connected a maximum of two other binary search subtrees of basic type B and for which the following must apply: the largest of all the nodes on the left subtree must have a value less than the root, which is in turn has a value less than the the nodes in the right subtree.

The binary tree represented above is also an example of a binary search tree. Character strings can be ordered alphabetically in the same way, such by last names:

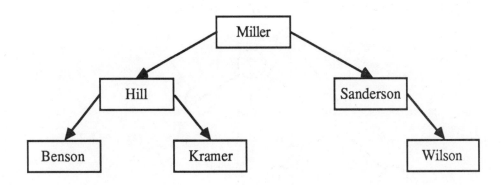

This data structure can be built in the main memory of a computer. In order to be able to put the tree structure on external storage media, you can use a *traversal procedure* to determine the order in which the nodes are stored.

2.1.1 Traversal procedure

In this section, we'll present three procedures for traversing (following the path) binary trees. In the examples, each node is identified by a single alphabetic character. The binary tree can thus be represented as a series of these identifying characters. The original binary tree can later be reconstructed from this series of characters.

Since it's possible to build a binary tree recursively, it's also possible to traverse (follow the path of) all of the nodes in the tree recursively as well. These three traversal procedures differ in the order in which they search the individual nodes of the tree. When a node does not have a successor (NIL pointer) this is indicated by a special character (here an asterisk *). All three procedures are explained with the help of the following tree:

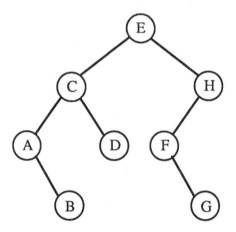

The first traversal procedure is called *pre-order* traversal. Here we start with the root, then proceed to the left subtree, and finish with the right subtree.

The pre-order traversal yields the following sequence:

```
E C A * B * * D * * H F * G * * *
```

This method of representing a binary tree can be formulated as a recursive procedure. The procedure preorderout uses the pre-order traversal. It writes the individual nodes and the NIL pointers (variable leaf is assigned a *) to a file (variable `source` of type `file of char`). When calling this procedure, a pointer (value parameter b of type `bintree`) to the root of the binary tree is passed.

```
procedure preorderout(b:bintree);

begin
  if b <> nil then
    begin
      write(source,b^.ident);
      preorderout(b^.left);
      preorderout(b^.right)
    end
  else write(source,leaf);
end;
```

The original tree can now be recreated recursively from the character string representation thereby preserving the pre-order sequence. The procedure `treeconstruct` performs this task only if the file in which this sequence is found is not empty (`filesize(source)<>0`). In this procedure, the internal function `preorderin` is used, which actually builds the binary tree. This function returns the reference to a new node or to a NIL element. The procedure passes the reference to the root (variable parameter `root`) of the binary tree to the outside.

If you are using Turbo Pascal with CP/M, you must activate the compiler directive **A** by entering (`{*$A-*}`) in order to properly execute the recursive procedure or function.

```
procedure treeconstruct(var root:bintree);

function preorderin:bintree;

var component : bintree
    k : char;

begin
  if not eof(source) then
    begin
      read(source,k);
      if k = character then preorderin:=nil
        else
          begin
            new(component);
```

```
            component^.ident:=k;
            component^.left:=preorderin;
            component^.rigt:=preorderin;
            preorderin:=component
         end;
     end
end;

begin
  reset(source);
  if filesize(source) <> 0 then root:=preorderin
end;
```

The second traversal method is called *in-order* traversal. With this method, you start with the left subtree, then the root and finally the right subtree.

The in-order traversal yields the following sequence:

```
      * A * B * C * D * E * F * G * H *
```

The procedure inorderout is a recursive implementation of this procedure. It has almost the same operation as the procedure preorderout (except for the order of the recursive procedure calls).

```
procedure inorderout(b:bintree);

begin
  if b <> nil then
    begin
      inorderout(b^.left);
      write(source,b^.ident);
      inorderout(b^.right)
    end
  else write(source,leaf)
end;
```

The in-order variant of the function preorderin can be implemented similarly to the previously described procedure treeconstruct.

The third traversal procedure is called *post-order* traversal. With this method, the traversal starts with the left subtree, then proceeds to the right subtree and finishes with the root.

The post-order traversal yields the following sequence:

```
* * * B A * * D C * * * G F * H E
```

The procedure postorderout is an implementation of this method. Its operation is similar to that of the procedure preorderout.

```
procedure postorderout(b:bintree);

begin
  if b <> nil then
    begin
      postorderout(b^.left);
      postorderout(b^.right);
      write(source,b^.ident)
    end
  else write(source,leaf)
end;
```

Here too, the function preorderin in the procedure treeconstruct can be changed according to the post-order traversal.

2.1.2 Operations with a binary tree

The structure of the binary tree is subject to many changes during the course of a program. Elements in this structure can be located, removed or inserted with little effort. In the following three sections we'll present these elementary operations and the algorithms that implement them.

2.1.2.1 Search

Locating an element in a set of data can be done efficiently only when the set is ordered. A binary search tree represents such an ordering in which the position of a given element can be found relatively quickly or it can be determined that the element does not exist.

The process of removing or inserting a node in the binary tree is always preceded by a search to find the node to be deleted or the position at which a node of its value shoud be inserted. Searching for an element in a binary search tree begins by comparing the element to be found with the value of the root of the tree. If the element to be found is greater than the root value, the search continues in the right subtree; otherwise it continues in the left subtree. The search is done when either the node with the same value as the element being searched for is found or a NIL element is found.

Here too, the search process can be formulated recursively. The procedure search is the implementation of this method:

```
procedure search(var b:bintree; x:char);

begin
  if b=nil then writeln(lst,'Element not present')
    else
      if x > b^.ident then search(b^.right,x)
        else
          if x < b^.ident then search(b^.left,x)
            else
              writeln(lst,'Element found');
end;
```

Using this procedure, you pass the root of the tree and the element to be searched for as parameters. If the element is not found in the tree (b = nil), an appropriate message is sent to the printer. If a match is found, a message to this effect is printed on the printer.

2.1.2.2 Insertion

In the procedure `treeconstruct` you can see the dynamic structure of the binary search tree. To allow the tree to grow, we require algorithms to insert an element. These algorithms must be developed so that the structure of the binary tree is preserved after the element is inserted.

Before we present the solution to this problem, let's look at one aspect of it: adding a leaf to a binary search tree. Let's assume that we want to insert the value O into a tree.

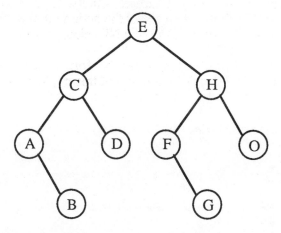

The insertion is preceded by a search. Once the parent (node H) of the new node is determined, the new leaf can be appended. The new leaf with the value O in our example, is inserted as the right child of the parent node.

The following procedure `append` is a recursive implementation of this process.

```
procedure append(var b:bintree; x:char);

begin
  if b = nil then
    begin
      new(b);
      b^.ident:=x;
```

```
        b^.left:=nil;
        b^.right:=nil;
      end
    else
      if x > b^.ident then append(b^.right,x)
        else
          if x < b^.ident then append(b^.left,x)
  end;
```

A reference to the root of the tree and the element to be appended is passed to this routine as parameters when it is called. Thanks to recursion, appending a leaf can be implemented quite elegantly.

Inserting a node requires somewhat more programming effort, since the procedure must be generalized to include both appending a leaf and inserting a node. Therefore the procedure must recognize each case.

```
procedure insert(b:bintree;x:char);

var c,component:bintree;
    ok:boolean;

begin
  c:=nil;
  ok:=false;
  while not ok do
    begin
      if b = nil then ok:=true
      else
        begin
          if x = b^.ident then ok:=true
            else
              begin
                c:=b;
                if x < b^.ident then b:=b^.left
                  else
                     b:=b^.right
              end
        end
    end;
  if b <> nil then writeln(lst,'Node already
                               present')
```

```
     else
       begin
         new(component);
         component^.ident:=x;
         component^.left:=nil;
         component^.right:=nil;
         if x < c^.ident then c^.left:=component
           else
             c^.right:=component
       end
end;
```

References to the root of the binary search tree and the element to be inserted are passed to the procedure `insert`. The insertion point is found iteratively in the **while**-loop of the procedure. If no node with the value of the element is present, a new node is created, initialized with the appropriate values and inserted at the designated point.

2.1.2.3 Deletion

Deleting an element from a binary search tree is a relatively complicated operation. After a node is removed from the tree, the structure of the tree must be put back together again. In contrast to insertion, this operation requires more effort. Deleting a leaf or a node with only one successor is not as complicated as deleting a node with two successors.

When removing a node with just one successor, the child reverts to the position of the parent. The following representation shows our binary search tree after the node A has been removed.

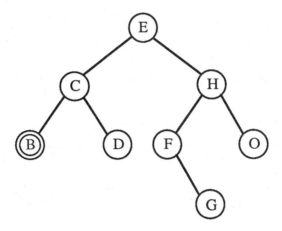

When removing a node with two successors, one of the following alternatives can be chosen: the deleted node is replaced either by the smallest node in the right subtree or by the largest node in the left subtree. We'll select the second alternative and demonstrate the operation of this method by removing the node E.

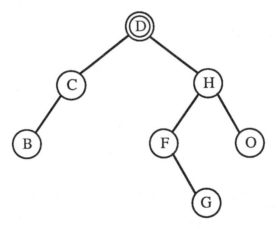

The structure of the binary search tree is retained as you can see. The choice of which alternative to use is up to you. The procedure `delete` is the implementation of this operation using the first method.

```
procedure delete(b:bintree;x:char);

var c : bintree;

procedure search(p:bintree; x:char);

begin
  if p=nil then writeln(lst,'Element not present')
    else
      if x > p^.ident then search(p^.right,x)
        else
          if x < p^.ident then search(p^.left,x)
            else
              b:=p;
end;

procedure two(var g:bintree);

begin
  if g^.right <> nil then two(g^.right)
    else
      begin
        c^.ident:=g^.ident;
        c:=g;
        g:=g^.left
      end
end;


begin
  search(b,x);
  c:=b;
  if c^.right = nil then b:=c^.left
    else
      if c^.left = nil then b:=c^.right
        else
          two(c^.left)
end;
```

A reference to the root of the tree and the element to be deleted are passed to the procedure delete. In this procedure, procedure search is called which finds the element to be deleted and returns a reference to it in the variable b. This element is then processed depending on the number of successors it has. If the node has two successors, the recursive procedure two is called. This second local procedure sets the value of the largest node in the left subtree equal to that of the node to be deleted and recreates the combination of the new node with its left subtree.

2.2 Balanced trees

Operations with binary search trees explained in the last sections can change this structure to a *degenerate* structure. By a degenerate binary search tree we mean a tree in which every node has only a left or right successor. The following shows a degenerate binary search tree:

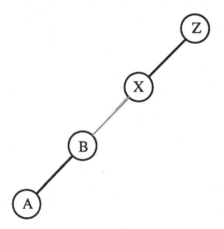

Searching for an element in a degenerate structure isn't very efficient. A lot of wasted effort is spent looking for a sucessor which is NIL. Degenerate structures occur seldomly, but when they do occur, they have a negative effect on the execution time of the operations.

The shortest search times are achieved when the height of the tree is as short as possible. Following this rule, you must develop a procedure which provides for the equal distribution of nodes to the left **and** right of the root. Such a tree is guaranteed to have an average search time of ln(n) time units.

If the number of nodes in the left subtree is different from the number of nodes in the right subtree by no more than one node, the tree is said to be *completely balanced.*

The following trees are completely balanced:

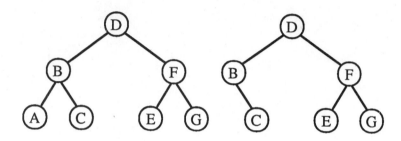

This structure is optimal for searching, but the effort required to rework the tree into this structure after each operation is considerable. Complete balancing requires so much work and is so slow that it should not be considered a workable technique.

2.2.1 AVL trees

An acceptable alternative to a completely balanced tree is the *balanced tree*. In a balanced tree, the height of the left subtree of each node differs from the height of its right subtree by at most one. This definition is less restrictive than the definition of the completely balanced tree.

The balanced tree was introduced by Adelson-Velskii and Landis in 1962 and since then has been named after them (*AVL tree*). A completely balanced tree is an AVL tree. On the other hand, not every AVL tree is a completely balanced tree. Adelson-Velskii and Landis determined that the balanced tree is a maximum of 45 percent higher than the completely balanced equivalent. The structure of the AVL tree guarantees a search time of ln(n) time units even in the worst case. In addition, it is much easier to balance the tree after a change.

The following representation shows a balanced AVL search tree which is not completely balanced.

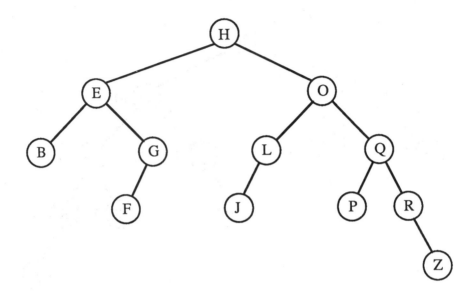

2.2.2 Operations with AVL trees

In order to efficiently balance a tree, the data structure node must be extended by one component. We will call this component the balance factor and for the sake of simplicity we will abbreviate it to bf. This component can, should the binary search tree be balanced, assume only the three values -1, 0, and +1. We have also changed ident to type char.

```
type node = record
              ident : char;
              bf : integer;
              left,right : bintree
            end;
```

The balance factor represents the allowable difference between the height of the left and right subtrees. The tree in the last figure is shown here with the new balance factors:

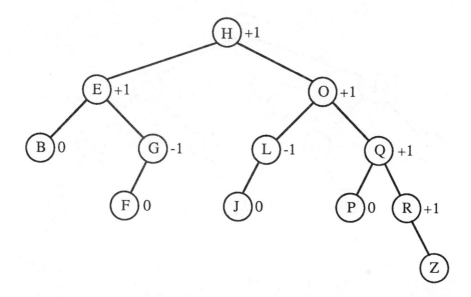

If the balance factor exceeds its balanced value (either less than -1 or greater than +1) after a node is inserted, the tree must be balanced from this node back towards the tree root.

Before a node can be inserted or deleted, it must be found in the tree. These operations always begin with a recursive search. During the search, a branch of the tree is constructed. The branch points back in the direction of the root. During this search, successive nodes of the branch are checked for the value of its balance factor. If necessary adjustments are made to balance the tree. To adjust the tree, several pointers are exchanged. Such an exchange is called a *rotation*. During rotation, the subtrees of a subtree are exchanged.

There are four different rotations. Depending on the condition of the tree, one of these four is used.

If the balance factor exceeds the value 1, then the relative height of the right subtree was increased during a previous operation. The tree can be re-balanced using a R-R (right-right) rotation. The following diagram illustrates this type of rotation (T indicates a subtree and the index beneath its height):

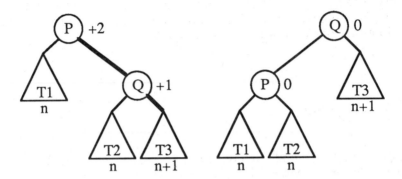

If the balance factor of a node increases because the height of the left subtree of the right subtree increased during an operation, the tree can be re-balanced with an RL (right-left) rotation. The following representation illustrates the RL rotation:

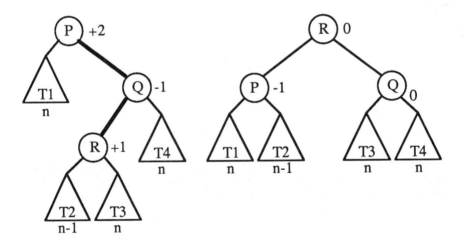

The LL (left-left) and LR (left-right) rotations are symmetric to the RR and RL rotations.

The properties of the search tree remain the same after each rotation.

Each change to the tree operates according to the same principle: first the node is inserted or deleted, then the tree is checked for balance and adjusted if necessary.

Searching for a node in an AVL search tree is no different from searching in a regular binary search tree. The procedure `search` in Section 2.1.2.1 can also be used for AVL search trees.

2.2.2.1 Insertion

After inserting a node in a balanced tree, a rotation must be performed in 50 percent of the cases. The next examples clarify these four operations on trees which have lost their AVL properties through the insertion of a node.

1) RR rotation

If inserting a node in the right subtree of a right subtree causes the loss of AVL properties, the RR rotation is used to restore the balance of the tree. Starting with the balanced binary search tree:

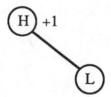

inserting a node with the value P increases the balance factor of the root of the tree by one. The new tree then loses its AVL characteristic and make an RR rotation necessary, which results in the following AVL tree:

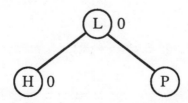

2) LL rotation

If a tree becomes unbalanced as the result of a node being inserted in the left subtree of a left subtree, an LL rotation is performed. This rotation is symmetrical to the RR rotation. Starting with the AVL search tree:

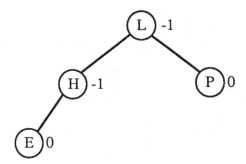

inserting node A requires an adjustment to the unbalanced tree. After the LL rotation the balanced search tree has the following structure:

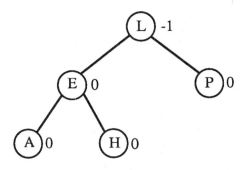

3) RL rotation

If you insert a node in the left subtree of a right subtree and this operation causes the loss of AVL properties, the RL rotation is necessary. Starting with the balanced tree:

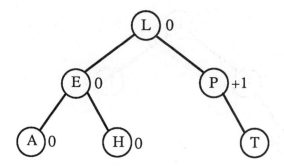

inserting a node with the value R causes the tree to lose its balance. In this case the RL rotation is used, which then converts this tree into a balanced search tree:

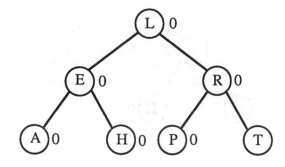

4) LR rotation

The last type of rotation is the LR rotation, which is the mirror image of the RL rotation. The LR rotation is performed when the tree becomes unbalanced as the result of inserting a node in the right subtree of a left subtree. Starting with the following balanced tree:

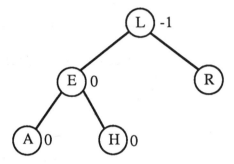

inserting a node with the value F destroys the balance of the tree. In this case the AVL characteristic of the tree can be restored with an LR rotation and the tree looks like this:

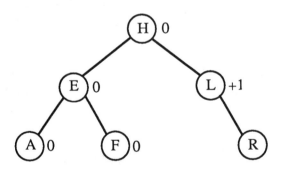

2.2.2.2 Deletion

After removing an element from a balanced tree, a tree loses it balance in about 20 percent of the cases. Deleting a node from an AVL tree is somewhat more complicated than insertion. The next four examples clarify the necessary balance operations.

1) RR rotation

Assume we start with the following balanced search tree:

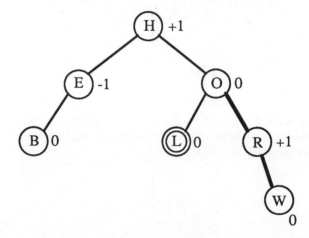

If you remove the node with the value L, the balance factor of the node with the value 0 indicates that an adjustment is required. In this case, the tree can be converted back to an AVL tree by performing an RR rotation.

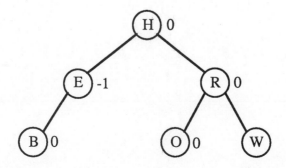

2) LL rotation

Starting with the balanced tree:

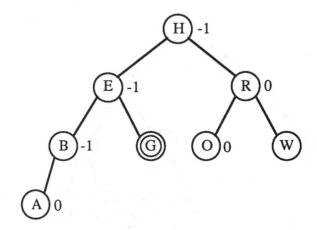

Deleting the node with the value G causes the tree to lose its balanced property. The tree can regain its AVL properties through an LL rotation, resulting in the following structure:

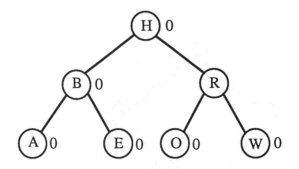

3) RL rotation

If you start with the following balance tree:

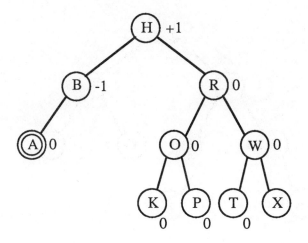

removing the node with the value A causes a loss of the AVL properties. After this operation the root of the search tree has a balance factor of +2. Through the RL rotation this tree recovers its balance and results in the following structure:

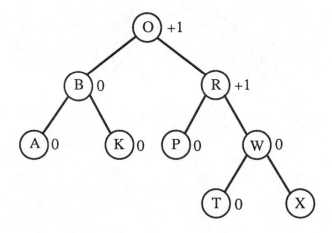

4) LR rotation

Starting with the AVL tree:

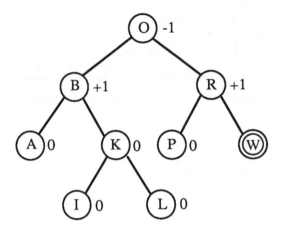

deleting the node with the value W leads to an imbalance which can be corrected by an LR rotation. The search tree has the following structure after the LR rotation:

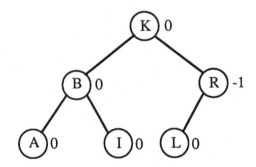

2.3 B-Trees

The binary search tree is generally built and managed in main memory. The size of this tree is determined primarily by the capacity of main memory. For larger applications, subtrees must be stored on external media and then loaded again as they are needed. Since accesses to an external storage medium such as a diskette or hard disk require a relatively large amount of time, this storage method is not very efficient. The concept of B-trees represents an optimal solution to the problem. The structure of the B-tree is conceived such that the number of disk accesses are kept to a minimum.

In a binary tree there is only a single key (element) in each node by which this node is identified. The nodes of a B-tree, on the other hand, contain multiple identifying keys. These nodes are also called *pages*.

A B-tree of order n can be defined as follows:

1. Each page contains a maximum of $2*n$ elements.

2. Each page, except for the root, contains at least n elements.

3. Each page which is not an end page (leaf), having k keys, has $k+1$ successors.

4. All end pages are found in one level.

From this definition you can conclude that any page other than the root page is used to at least 50 percent of full capacity. The result of this is that the maximum number of disk accesses for a B-tree of order n with x elements is $\log_{n+1}(x)$.

The next figure shows a B-tree of order 2. Except for the root page, which consists of only one element, each page contains at least two but no more than four elements. A page which contains two elements has three successors.

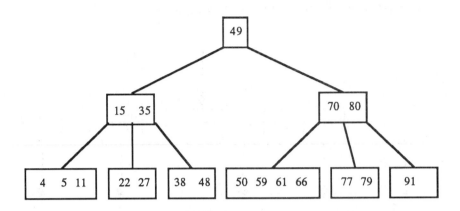

This B-tree is also a search tree. Preceeding and following each element of a page is a pointer which points to a successor page. The pointer preceeding a given element x, points to a successor page which contains elements all less than x. The pointer following element x, points to another successor page which contains elements all greater than those which x contains.

Before we develop the algorithm for a B-tree of order n, we should first define the structure of a page. In addition to the maximum of $2*n$ elements, we need $2*n+1$ pointers. The data structure page can be declared as follows:

```
type page = ^spage;
     element = record
                  ident : integer;
                  refs : page;
               end;


type spage = record
               a : array[1..2*n] of element;
               index : 0..2*n;
               ver : page
             end;
```

Every page of a B-tree has the following form:

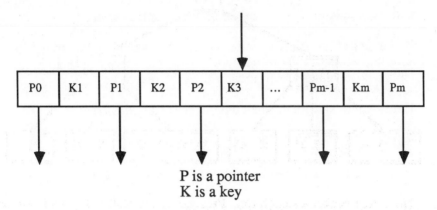

P is a pointer
K is a key

This applies for n≤m≤2*n. The linear order of the keys on a page, that is K1<K2<...<Km, is suited for a linear or binary search.

2.3.1 Operations with B-trees

The operations on binary trees cannot be easily transferred to B-trees. Searching for, inserting into and deleting an element from the B-tree is a completely different problem. In this section, we'll take a closer look at these operations.

2.3.1.1 Search

The search for a specific key in a B-tree begins at the root. In our example, the root has only one element. The initial search has one of three outcomes: a) the search key matches the root element; b) the search key has a value less than the root key; c) the search key has a value greater than the root.

If the search key matches the root element, then we are done. We have successfully completed the search.

If the search key has a value less than that of the root, then we must follow one of the pointers to one of the successor pages. In this case, the pointer which preceeds the root key points to the sucessor page containing elements whose values are all less than the search key.

If the search key has a value greater than that of the root, then the pointer which follows the root key points to the successor page containing elements whose values are all greater than the search key.

Here's an illustration of the contents of a simple B-tree:

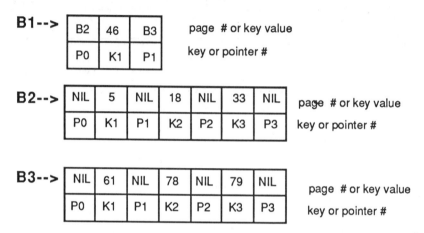

It contains three records (B1, B2 and B3). Record B1 is the root. In each of the blocks are varying number of elements. There are a maximum of 2*n keys (K0..Kn) and 2*n+1 pointers (P0..Pn)

Consider a search key of 18. In our example, the root key value is 46. Since the search key is less than the root key value, we would follow the pointer which preceeds the root value (P0 in B1) which points to B2. Next the search value is compared to each key in B2. We find a match when comparing the search key with K2 or B2. So the search is successful.

If the search key were 36, we would attempt to follow pointer P3 in B2. But it is NIL, so we know that search key 36 doesn't exist.

The search is continued on this page until either the key is found or until the end page reached and the element is still not found.

The maximum search length depends on the depth of the B-tree. If the end pages are on the kth level, the search length will have a maximum of k page references. The determining factor is the order of the B-tree. By way of example, during the search of a B-tree of order 256 with 100,000 elements, a maximum of three page accesses are necessary.

2.3.1.2 Insertion

Inserting an element into a B-tree is relatively simple. If there are fewer than $2*n$ elements on a page, the element need only be inserted at the appropriate point. Starting with the B-tree:

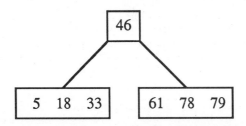

inserting an element with the value 75 would lead to the following B-tree:

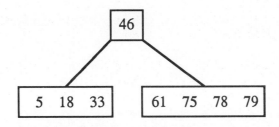

Inserting an element into a page which already has $2*n$ elements is considerably more complicated. This situation is referred to as *overflow*. In this case, the elements on the page are divided into two pages. The first n elements are put on the left page and the last n on the right and the n+1st element is put on the predecessor page. This process is called *splitting*.

Splitting a page may cause an overflow on the predecessor page, making it necessary to split this page as well. In the worst case, when all pages are filled with 2*n elements, the overflow can lead back to the root of the B-tree. The root page is then split into two pages. The n+1st element are placed in the new root of the B-tree. In this manner the B-tree grows continually from bottom to top. Splitting a page when overflow occurs and the upward growth of the tree guarantee that it retains its B-tree characteristics (balance).

Inserting an element with the value 64 in the previous example leads to overflow in the right page. This page is then split into two pages. The elements with the values 61 and 64 go to one page and the elements with the values 78 and 79 go to the other. The middle element with the value 75 is inserted in the root page:

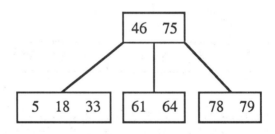

2.3.1.3 Deletion

The process of deletion is more complicated and correspondingly more difficult to describe than insertion. Removing an element from an end page is relatively simple, as long as the page contains more than n elements. In this case, the element and the pointer following it are simply removed from the page. If there are only n elements on the end page, then removing an element leads to an *underflow*. Underflow means that a page has fewer than n nodes. We must distinguish between two cases when handling underflow:

1. The neighboring page on the right (right brother) contains more than n elements. In this case, the operation balance can be performed. The process of balancing is carried out between the two brothers. The effect of this operation does not change the degree of branching

of the parent.

When balancing, the key element found between the two pointers pointing to the page in question is first removed from the parent page and sorted into the left son page, meaning that it becomes the largest element on this page. The first pointer (here a NIL pointer) of the right page becomes the last pointer on the left page. The smallest (first) element on the right son page is removed and inserted into the parent page. In this manner the B-tree characteristics are retained.

Deleting key 22 from this B-tree:

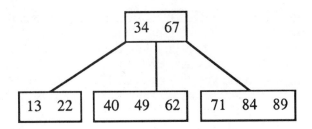

leads to an underflow in the left son. With the help of the procedure described above, we can correct the underflow condition by balancing so that the tree regains its B-tree properties. The key 34 is inserted into the left son and the key 40 takes its place.

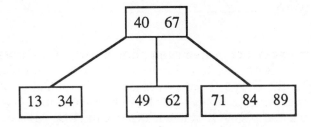

This procedure can be also be reversed which is equivalent to balancing the son page by removing the first element of the next right neighbor. The underflow is corrected by removing the largest element from the next left neighbor page.

2. It's possible that no neighboring page has more than n elements. Then the operation merge must be used to combine the contents of one page with that of its neighboring page, thereby forming a single page.

If the underflow occurred in page x, the key and pointer following the pointer to page x are removed from the parent page. This key is inserted into the son page x at the nth position. The last NIL pointer of the page now at the n+1st position. All elements from the next right neighbor page are inserted in page x following this pointer. This operation can also lead to a underflow which can in turn propogate back to the root page.

For example, if we remove key 34 from the previous diagram, we can correct the B-tree by merging the left and middle leaf pages. Underflow occurs in the left page when the element is deleted. By merging, the key 40 is removed from the parent page and inserted in the left son page with the keys 49 and 62. The pointer to the middle leaf page is removed. After this merge procedure the B-tree has the following form:

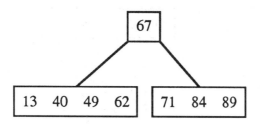

Removing an element from a page that is not an end or leaf page is somewhat different. The deleted key is replaced with the next largest key of the B-tree. The next largest key is found by following the next pointer and the first pointer of all following child pages until this leads to a leaf page. Once at a leaf page, the first key is removed and inserted in the page in question.

If you delete key 55 from the root of the following B-tree (partial section):

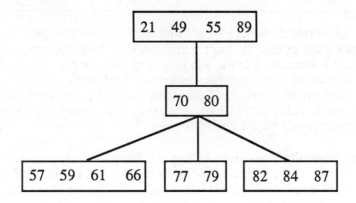

then the key 57 is inserted into the root page. After this operation the B-tree again has a balanced structure:

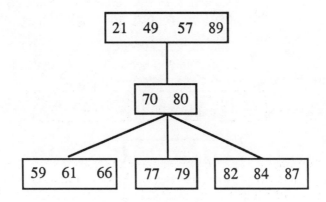

Removing a key from the end page can lead to underflow, making it necessary to use balancing as described above to correct the situation.

2.3.2 B-trees and databases

The most common application of B-trees is found in database and information systems. In this section we'll present an overview of the structure of these systems. This should make it easier for you to use the Turbo Toolbox package developed by Borland International.

These applications examples are concerned with the most efficient storage and retrieval process possible. The speed of this process depends on the basic search procedure used. Up to this point in our discussion of B-trees, both the key element and the associated data were assumed to be stored in each page. Depending on the amount of this data, the size of a page could be enormous.

Moving the data of a large-sized page from disk to main memory requires a relatively large amount of processing time. Disk to main memory transfer is slow. In searching for information, the majoritiy of the time only the key component is used. One way to make B-trees more efficient is to place only key of the record in the pages (a key-tree). The remainder of the data record is then stored in an arbitrary position in a random-access file. This key-tree is a B-tree in which every element of a page contains the key component and the position (record address) of the record in the random-access file.

For a simple card catalog file you need a record consisting of five fields: author, title, keyword, publisher and copyright date.

Here's a sample card catalog:

| Author |
| Title |
| Keyword |
| Publisher |
| Copyright date |

Each data record in the file has this structure. From this set of selected data (five different fields) we can select one field and declare it to be the key (such as author). These data records can be accessed using this key. In practice, the data record is first initialized with the five items and placed in a random-access file at a specific record address. The key and the record address are then inserted into a key tree as one element. When looking for literature - a book, a magazine or an article - you can search for it by using this key (name of the author). This resembles a card catalog in a library where the books are ordered according to author.

When removing a record, only the corresponding key and record address is removed from the search tree. The data record remains in the file. The user can no longer access it because the key and the record address no longer exist in the key tree. At specific intervals, as determined by the number of deletions made, the file must be reorganized. Reorganization prevents the waste of space occupied by these "deleted" records in the random file.

A card catalog system which can be searched by only one key is not very useful. A complete system allows for search author, title, keyword, etc. Searching on multiple keys is also very useful in other applications. Up until now we have assumed that each key can be assigned to one data record.

Three keys are more useful for a card catalog system: author, title and keyword (subject). A query of such a system might require that all literature written by a specific author be printed. The following small database is intended to demonstrate the entire data inventory of a literature information system:

#	Author	Title	Keyword	Publisher	Date
1	Aho,J. Ullman,	Prin. of Compiler	compilers	Addison-Wesley	1977
2	Date, C.J.	Database: A Primer	data bases	Addison-Wesley	1981
3	Kernighan, B Plauger,	Software Tools	utilities	Addison-Wesley	1976
4	Knuth, D.	Sorting & Searching	files, sorting	Addison-Wesley	1973
5	Wirth, N	Systemat	Pascal	Prentice-Hall	1978
6	Wiederhold, G	Database Design	data bases	McGraw-Hill	1977
7	Martin, J	Computer Database Organization	data bases	Prentice-Hall	1975
8	Wirth, N	Algorithm, Data	programming	Prentice-Hall	1976

The order of the records is not important here. In our system, any record can be identified by the three keys: author, title and keyword. A separate search tree must be built for each of these keys. The record's address in the random access file must also be kept in the three B-trees. Removing a record requires changes to all three search trees. These changes become more costly as the number of keys increases.

A query of our information system for the author with the name *Wirth, N* would return the contents of data record 5 and 8 as the result. A query for the keyword *data bases* would return the contents of records 2, 6 and 7. As the number of data records increases, so does the number of records that can be identified with a given key.

Professional database and catalog systems offer more search keys per book than our simple system. Our example system could be expanded to include multiple authors of a single book, for example. The same structure could be used to allow multiple keywords.

Queries can have a much more complicated form. For example: search for all books on computers which were written between 1972 and 1982. Before we decide how to implement a complex query system, you should know something about the basic concepts of this system. The rest of this section is a brief overview of the design of such systems.

A database system must be designed so that it can stand up to continual changes in its structure. Such a system must also support subsequent changes such as the addition of new fields, removing unneeded fields, changing the contents or characteristics of an existing field, and so on.

A database structure should be developed independent of the data so that any reorganization of the data require minimal changes to the programs that use the database. To ensure this, the strict dependencies between the user program and the data organization must be removed. The database system makes the data available to the user in the way he organized it. The user sees a logical file whose structure does not correspond to the physical organization of data in memory or on disk. The conversion of the physical format into the logical is organized by the corresponding database software.

The architecture of database systems can be described by the following three-level model:

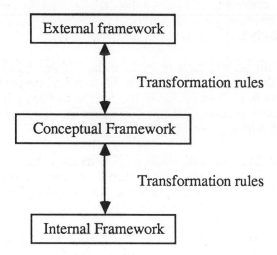

Multiple users can communicate with the database system by using user-friendly languages through an external framework. The conceptual framework forms the basis for development of the other frameworks. This framework comprises the application independent description of the data and represents a summary of the logical level of the system. The internal framework describes the physical storage of data on disk. The transformation rules make the connections and relationships between the objects of the conceptual and the internal of external model.

In database systems, data and their relationshops are described independent of the program through *data models*. The three major data models are: the *network*, the *hierarchical* and the *relational*. A data model is a formal description of data (fields, records, bases, etc.) and how they relate to each other. On a higher level, a data model is a reproduction of an existing structure in our real world. The data model does not describe not the physical structure of the data (how the data is stored in files).

As an example of this structure, we take the organization chart of a company. The three different data models are explained using this example.

1) The network data model

The objects of this data model are connected to each other in the form of a network. The following structure descibes the connection between an employee, his department, and his salary:

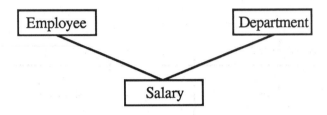

2) The hierarchical data model

The hierarchical organization structure of a firm is well suited for this model. The following representation describes the tree-like organization of a company by function:

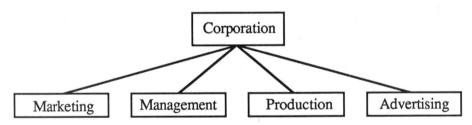

3) The relational data model

   The relational model is best for systematic representation of data and its subsequent independent representation by another application. The data are represented in the form of tables. In our example, the person-specific data for every employee can be organized in a table:

Last name	First name	Department	Position	Age
Jones	Tom	Advertising	Dept. director	45
Smith	Jane	Management	Secretary	23
Harrison	John	Production	Operator	29

   Of the three data models, the most prevalent are the network and relational models.

   Powerful database systems offer an easy-to-use and efficient interface to the user in the form of a database language. This language is dependent on the data model chosen. With the help of these languages, non-programmers can work with database systems with relatively little effort.

CHAPTER 3

Chapter 3: Turbo Pascal and the Operating System

This section is an introduction to accessing the operating system facilities from Turbo Pascal. Since there are two major implementations of Turbo Pascal, we'll separate the discussions into the facilities of CP/M and MS-DOS.

3.1 CP/M-80

CP/M-80 is an operating system designed for the 8080 and Z-80 processors. The CP/M operating system is made up of three major parts:

BIOS (Basic Input/Output System)
Part of the operating system that performs all of the physical or hardware dependent tasks. It is essentially the software interface between the computer peripherals and the rest of the operating system.

BDOS (Basic Disk Operating System)
Part of the operating system that handles the logical input and ouptut tasks.It performs the logical transfer of data between the computer and peripherals, independent of the physical characteristics of that peripheral. By separating the logical characteristics of the device from the physical characteristics, the user's software does not have to change to access the when the devices are changed. For example if a 5-1/4" drive replaces an 8" drive in a computer system, the application program does not have to be changed to access the new peripheral.

CCP (Console Command Processor)
Part of the operating system that interprets the commands typed at the keyboard.

Turbo Pascal has several built-in procedures and functions that let you communicate with the BIOS and BDOS to perform specific tasks.

3.1.1   CP/M BDOS Routines

The BDOS is an interface between the user and the different hardware devices. All of the data transfer to and from the peripherals take place over this interface. CP/M is organized so that a number of standardized routines to perform specific functions are available to the programmer. By using these routines you can access the devices without having to concern yourself with the hardware characteristics of the computer system.

Turbo Pascal lets you access these routines using the standard procedure `Bdos`:

```
Bdos(function_number,parm);
```

You can also access these routines using the standard functions `Bdos` and `BdosHL`. The routines return values in either the A register or the HL register pair. This is the reason for the two different functions:

```
var := Bdos(function_number,parm);
```
returns the integer result in the A register

```
var := BdosHL(function_number,parm);
```
returns the value in HL register pair

Both `function_number` and the `parm` are of type `integer`. Specifying `parm` is optional and depends on the particular BDOS routine called.

Here is a list of the major BDOS routines:

0. Warm start

This routine returns control of the computer to the CP/M operating system.

```
procedure Warmstart;

begin
  Bdos(0)
end;
```

1. Console input

Reads the next character from the console into the A register.

```
procedure ConsoleInput;

var x : integer;

begin
  x:=Bdos(1)
end;
```

The ASCII value of the key that was pressed is assigned to variable x. The corresponding character is displayed on the screen if it is printable. This routine and the statement read(trm,x) (where x is a character variable) are identical.

2. Console output

The character in the E register is sent to the console device.

```
procedure ConsoleOutput;

var x : integer;

begin
  x:=42;
  Bdos(2,x)
end;
```

This procedure ConsoleOutput prints an "*" on the screen (CHR(42)).

5. List output

The character contained in the E register is send to the list device (printer). It is used the same way as ConsoleOutput above.

13. Disk reset

The character in the E register is sent to the console device.

```
procedure DiskReset;

begin
    Bdos(13)
end;
```

Resets the disk file system. All of the drives are set to read/write, drive A is selected and the file control blocks are reinitialized.

The other BDOS routine calls require a detailed understanding of the CP/M operating system which is not the intent of this book. If you are interested in more information, we direct you to the bibliography.

3.1.2   CP/M BIOS Routines

The BIOS is the hardware dependent part of the operating system. The routines in the BIOS are adapted to the exact hardware configuration of the computer. The BIOS consists of many short routines which the BDOS uses to access the peripherals.

Turbo Pascal lets you access these routines also by using the standard procedure Bios.

```
        Bios(function_number,parm);
```

You can also access these routines using the standard functions Bios and BiosHL.

```
        var := Bios(function_number,parm);
                    returns integer result in A register
        var := BiosHL(function_number,parm);
                    returns value in HL register pair
```

Both `function_number` and `parm` are of type `integer`. `Function_number` and `parm` (optional depending on routine) are used in the same manner as for `Bdos`, although the function numbers are different.

Here's a partial list of BIOS routines:

0. Warm start

```
procedure Warmstart;

begin
  Bios(0)
end;
```

1. Console status

```
procedure ConsoleStatus;

var kp: integer;

begin
  kp := Bios(1);    {kp=0, no key pressed }
end;                {kp=255, key pressed  }
```

2. Console input

3. Console output

4. List output

The other BIOS routines are described in other CP/M literature.

3.2 MS-DOS and PC-DOS

PC-DOS is a powerful operating system for the IBM PC. MS-DOS is essentially the same operating system as PC-DOS for IBM PC compatible computers such as the COMPAQ. From this point on, we'll refer to both of these as MS-DOS since it is a more generic term.

MS-DOS is made up of five major parts:

BOOT LOADER
>   A short program kept in the first sector of the diskette. It's job is to "boot" or load the rest of the operating system when the PC is first turned on or reset.

ROM BIOS (Basic Input/Output System in Read-Only-Memory)
>   Part of the operating system which performs the most fundamental tasks for the keyboard, screen display, disk drive, communication port, printer and other peripherals. The routines of the ROM BIOS are permanently stored in the Read-Only-Memory chips on the PC's main circuit board.

IBMBIO.COM (Basic Input/Output System)
>   Part of the operating system that performs the physical or hardware dependent tasks not found in the ROM BIOS. This part of the operating system may be extended (with device drivers) to handle specific peripherals that are attached to the computer. Together the ROM BIOS and the IBMBIO make up the physical part of MS-DOS.

IBMDOS.COM (Disk Operating System)
>   Part of the operating system that handles the logical input and ouput tasks. Tasks such as managing a disk directory, reading data from a diskette or determining the amount of available space on a diskette are performed by the DOS.

COMMAND.COM
>   Part of the operating system that interprets the commands that are typed at the keyboard.

MS-DOS provides various routines that are accessible to the programmer. These services may be accessed by *interrupts*. The IBM PC has a total of 256 different interrupts. The first 16 are hardware interrupts and are not of interest to us here. The rest are called software interrupts. Depending on which interrupt is generated, the computer performs the routine pointed to by *vectors* or 4-byte addresses located at fixed locations in memory.

3.2.1 INTR Using the Interrupt Routines

The routines of the ROM BIOS and DOS can be called from Turbo Pascal by using the standard procedure INTR.

```
INTR(interrupt_number,registers);
```

The first parameter specified the interrupt number and is of type integer.

The second parameter must be of type:

```
record
    AX,BX,CX,DX,BP,SI,DI,DS,ES,Flags : integer;
end;
```

and represents the individual 16-bit registers in the 8088 CPU.

Certain values must be placed in the registers depending on the routine being accessed. For example, interrupt 37 (hex 25) is used to read disk sectors. Before calling this routine using the INTR procedure, the following information must be passed through the appropriate registers:

Register	Contents
BS	memory address for data
AL	drive number index 0=Drive A,1=Drive, etc.
DX	starting sector number 0=1st sector,1=2nd sector, etc.
CS	number of sectors to read

At the conclusion of the interrupt, information is passed back through the registers. This information pertains to the status of the services that were performed.

For example, the read disk sector interrupt (interrupt 37) returns the status in the AL register:

Code	Meaning
12	general, non-specific error
11	read error
8	sector not found
7	disk format not recognized
6	seek error
4	CRC error
2	drive not ready
1	invalid drive number

In addition, further information is passed back in the AH register. You can consult one of the references in the bibliography for more detailed information.

A few tricks are needed to place information into the registers using Turbo Pascal.

The contents of the most-significant byte of a register must be placed into the register before the least-significant byte. To do this, we use the SHL operator. SHL shifts an integer number to the left, bit by bit. The number of bits to shift is user specified. For example:

```
res := 1 SHL 8;
```

shifts the number 1 eight bits to the left and assigns the resulting value 256 to variable res.

In binary representation, the whole thing looks like this:

0000000000000001	binary representation of the integer number 1 before the shift.
0000000100000000	binary representation of the result, 256, after shifting 8-bits to the left

During a shift, a zero-bit is automatically inserted into the rightmost position.

If an integer value is viewed as individuals bytes, the most-significant byte contains the value 1 and the least-significant byte contains the value 0. With `SHL 8` we have shifted the number 1 into the high-order byte. We'll use this method in all routines to set the high-order byte of a 16-bit register.

Sometimes it's necessary to separate the bytes of a 16-bit register. Turbo Pascal has two standard functions for doing this `HI` and `LO`. The high-order byte can be determined by using function `HI` and the low-order byte with the function `LO`. For example:

```
HiByte := HI(AX);
LoByte := LO(AX);
```

3.2.2 MsDos - Using DOS interrupt 33

There is a second Turbo Pascal standard procedure for accessing certain routines of MS-DOS. This standard procedure is called, simply enough, `MsDos`.

In contrast to `INTR`, the `MsDos` procedure requires only one parameter - the same type as the second parameter of the INTR procedure:

```
record
    AX,BX,CX,DX,BP,SI,DI,DS,ES,Flags : integer;
  end;
```

When `MsDos` standard procedure is called, Turbo Pascal generates interrupt 33 (hex 21).

Using: `MsDos(regs);` is equivalent to: `INTR($21,regs);`

By using the `MsDos` standard procedure, you can access the DOS service routines that are also available as separate interrupt services. However, most IBM reference literature caution you to access the DOS services only though interrupt 33 (hex 21), and not through their equivalent individual interrupts.

CHAPTER 4

Chapter 4: MS-DOS Extended Screen Output Routines

4.1 User-definable *cursor*

The cursor is actually made up of individual horizontal lines. In turn, a horizontal line is a series of individual pixels on the screen. A cursor can be defined as a different number of lines depending on the current text mode (BW = monochrome, C = color):

Monochrome (black and white/BW) mode: 14 lines
Color mode: 8 lines

The lines are numbered from top to bottom (0-13 or 0-7). The appearance of the cursor can be changed using the following procedure. The parameters specify the line numbers. The first parameter is the starting line number and the second parameter the ending line number.

Save to disk under the name **cursor**

```
1     procedure cursor(ch,cl:byte);
2
3     type regtype = record
4                         ax,bx,cx,dx,bp,
5                         di,si,ds,es,flags : integer;
6                    end;
7
8     var register : regtype;
9         ah       : byte;
10
11    begin
12        ah := 1;
13
14        with register do
15          begin
16            ax := ah shl 8;
17            cx := ch shl 8 + cl;
18            intr($10,register);
19          end;
20    end;
```

The procedure cursor calls a ROM BIOS routine which is responsible for displaying the cursor. The starting line is placed in ch register and the ending line in cl register. DOS interrupt 16 (hex 10) is called with function 1 passed through the cl register.

Examples:

The call

```
cursor(0,7);
```

causes the cursor to appear as a rectangle. The cursor can be completely suppressed with

```
cursor(8,0);
```

To create a one-line cursor with the line in the middle of the character matrix, we call the procedure cursor as follows:

```
cursor(4,4);
```

4.2 Multiple page screen output

4.2.1 *Page* procedure

The IBM PC with a color graphics card has the ability to work with multiple screen pages. The number of pages depends on the active text mode.

In the text mode C40 (40 columns per line), there are 8 screen pages available while in the C80 text mode (80 columns per line), there are 4 screen pages available. The pages are numbered from 0 to 7 (C40) or 0 to 3 (C80).

The individual pages (including those not currently visible) can be written to, but only one can be displayed at a time. The active page can be set by using the procedure Page and specifying the page number.

Save to disk under the name **page.prc**

```
1    procedure Page(al : byte);
2
3    type regtype = record
4                      ax,bx,cx,dx,bp,
5                      di,si,ds,es,flags : integer;
6                   end;
7
8    var register : regtype;
9        ah       : byte;
10
11   begin
12       ah := 5;
13
14       with register do
15          begin
16             ax := ah shl 8 + al;
17             intr($10,register);
18          end;
19   end;
```

DOS interrupt 16 (hex 10) is called with function 5 passed through the ah register and the page number passed through the ah register (line 16).

Example:

After turning the computer on, screen page 0 is always active. In order to change this and activate page 2, for example, the procedure Page is called as follows:

```
Page(1);
```

4.2.2 *WhichPage* function

The number of the active page can be determined by using this function. The active page is the one currently visible.

Individual pages are numbered as described in Section 4.2.1.

Text mode C40 with pages 0 to 7
Text mode C80 with pages 0 to 3

Save to disk under the name **wpage.fnc**

```
1     function WhichPage : byte;
2
3     type regtype = record
4                       ax,bx,cx,dx,bp,
5                       di,si,ds,es,flags : integer;
6                   end;
7
8     var register : regtype;
9         ah           : byte;
10
11    begin
12        ah := 15;
13
14        with register do
15          begin
16            ax := ah shl 8;
17            intr($10,register);
18            WhichPage := hi(bx);
19          end;
20    end;
```

DOS interupt 16 (hex 10) is called with function 15 passed through the ah register. The page number is returned in the high order byte of the bx register.

Example:

The call:

```
page := WhichPage;
```

returns the active page number in the variable page.

4.2.3 *GotoSXY* procedure

This procedure lets you positions the cursor to a given line, column, and page.

After positioning the cursor, you can use the procedure `print` to write character to the screen pages, even though they are not visible.

Note that the standard procedure `Write` and `Writeln` write characters to page 0 only.

The lines are numbered from 0 to 24. The number of columns is dependent on the current text mode:

Mode	Column numbers	Page numbers
C40	0 to 39	0 to 7
C80	0 to 79	0 to 3

Save to disk under the name **gotosxy.prc**

```
1    procedure GotoSXY(bh,dl,dh : byte);
2
3    type regtype = record
4                     ax,bx,cx,dx,bp,
5                     di,si,ds,es,flags : integer;
6                 end;
7
8    var register : regtype;
9        ah        : byte;
10
11   begin
12       ah := 2;
13
14       with register do
15         begin
16           ax := ah shl 8;
17           bx := bh shl 8;
18           dx := dh shl 8 + dl;
19           intr($10,register);
20         end;
21   end;
```

Examples:

```
GotoSXY(2,10,20);
```

positions the cursor in the eleventh column of the twenty-first line on the third page.

```
GotoSXY(0,3,4);   is identical to:   GotoXY(4,5);
```

4.2.4 *WhereSX, WhereSY* functions

The functions WhereSX and WhereSY are comparable to the standard functions WhereX and WhereY, except that the page number is used.

The page number (0 to 3 or 0 to 7) is passed as a function argument. The functions returns the current cursor position on the given page.

The lines are numbered from 0 to 24 and the columns from 0 to 79 or 0 to 39 (for WhereX and WhereY the numbering starts with 1).

Save to disk under the name **wheresx.fnc**

```
1     function WhereSX(bh : byte) : byte;
2
3     type regtype = record
4                        ax,bx,cx,dx,bp,
5                        di,si,ds,es,flags : integer;
6                    end;
7
8     var register : regtype;
9         ah          : byte;
10
11    begin
12        ah := 3;
13
```

```
14        with register do
15           begin
16              ax := ah shl 8;
17              bx := bh shl 8;
18              intr($10,register);
19              whereSX := lo(dx);
20           end;
21   end;
```

Save to disk under the name **wheresy.fnc**

```
1    function WhereSY(bh : byte) : byte;
2
3    type regtype = record
4                     ax,bx,cx,dx,bp,
5                     di,si,ds,es,flags : integer;
6                   end;
7
8    var register : regtype;
9        ah       : byte;
10
11   begin
12        ah := 3;
13
14        with register do
15           begin
16              ax := ah shl 8;
17              bx := bh shl 8;
18              intr($10,register);
19              whereSY := hi(dx);
20           end;
21   end;
```

DOS interrupt 16 (hex 10) is called with function 3 passed through the ah register and the page number passed through the bh register.

The result is returned in the dx register. The line number is in the high-order byte and the column number is in the low-order byte. The appropriate value is returned in the function variable in line 19.

To determine the line position of the cursor on page 2, for example, the function `WhereSY` is called as follows:

```
line := WhereSY(1);
```

The cursor position in the current page can be found with the call:

```
line := WhereSY(WhichPage);
column := WhereSX(WhichPage);
```

4.3 Controlling the screen through attributes

4.3.1 *Print* procedure

This procedure outputs characters to the screen. A special feature of `Print` is its ability to send characters to any page, including those not visible. In addition, the appearance of the characters can be specified by using attributes.

The characters are placed on the screen beginning at the current cursor position. This may be set using procedure `GotoSXY`.

Procedure `Print` is called with three parameters. The first parameter determines the page to which the characters will be sent. The second parameter specifies the appearance of the characters. The third parameter is the character string itself.

The following table contains a list of codes that may be used to specify a character string's attributes with the `Print` procedure.

Code	Attribute	Effect
1	$01	underline
2	$07	normal
3	$09	underline and emphasized
4	$70	inverse
5	$71	underline, not reversed
6	$78	inverse and emphasized
7	$79	underline and emphasized
8	$81	underline with flash
9	$87	normal flash
10	$89	underline flash and emphasized
11	$F0	inverse flash
12	$F8	inverse flash and emphasized

Procedure `Print` uses the functions `WhereSX` and `WhereSY` and the procedure `GotoSXY`. These must be previously defined in a program using `Print` (Sections 4.2.3 and 4.2.4).

Save to disk under the name **print.prc**

```
1    procedure Print(bh,bl:byte;var wt);
2
3    type regtype = record
4                       ax,bx,cx,dx,bp,
5                       di,si,ds,es,flags : integer;
6                   end;
7
8    var register : regtype;
9        ah,al,lf : byte;
10       sg,os    : integer;
11
12   begin
13
14     if (bl>=1) and (bl<=12) and
15        (bh>=0) and (bh<=3) then
16        begin
17          ah := 9;
18          sg := seg(wt);
19          os := ofs(wt);
20
```

```
21            case bl of
22                1 : bl := $01;   {U}
23                2 : bl := $07;   {N}
24                3 : bl := $09;   {U,E}
25                4 : bl := $70;   {I}
26                5 : bl := $71;   {U}
27                6 : bl := $78;   {I,E}
28                7 : bl := $79;   {E,U}
29                8 : bl := $81;   {B,U}
30                9 : bl := $87;   {B,N}
31               10 : bl := $89;   {B,U,E}
32               11 : bl := $f0;   {B,I}
33               12 : bl := $f8;   {B,I,E}
34            end;
35
36            with register do
37              begin
38                cx := 1;
39                bx := bh shl 8 + bl;
40
41                for lf := 1 to mem[sg:os] do
42                  begin
43                    al := mem[sg:os+lf];
44                    ax := ah shl 8 + al;
45                    intr($10,register);
46
47                    if WhereSX(bh)=79 then
48                       GotoSXY(bh,0,WhereSY(bh)+1)
49                    else
50                       GotoSXY(bh,WhereSX(bh)+1,
                                    WhereSY(bh))
51                  end;
52              end;
53            end;
54  end;
```

Lines 14 and 15 check the range of the input parameters. The page number bh may be between 0 and 3. For 40-column screen representation (text mode C40), the maximum allowable page can be changed to 7. The attribute number in bl is allowed to be between 1 to 12.

In lines 18 and 19, the address of the string variable (third parameter) is placed in sg (segment) and os (offset). In lines 21 through 34 the attribute number in bl is replaced by the corresponding attribute.

The IBM PC recognizes more than these twelve attributes. We have selected only those which seem the most useful. If you want to add other attributes to the table, we refer you to the appropriate MS-DOS literature in the bibliography.

In line 38 the register cx is set to the number of times that each character is to be written (only once).

The page number in bh and the attribute in bl are transferred to the low-order byte of register bx (line 39).

Within the **for**-loop which runs from 1 to the length of the string, the individual characters of the string are written to the screen. DOS interrupt 16 (hex 10) is called with function 9 passed in the ah register (line 17) and the character to be written is passed in the al register. The string length is obtained by using the Mem function. The first byte of the string contains the string length.

The cursor position is set in the if statement (lines 47-50) since the ROM BIOS function does not change the cursor position.

CHAPTER 5

5. *Input* Function - for easy input

5.0 Introduction

The methods of inputting data from the keyboard are rather limited in Turbo Pascal.

The standard procedures `Read` and `Readln` allow inputting of characters, but without special editing capabilities. Characters can be deleted with the backspace key during the input or entire lines can be deleted with `Ctrl-X`. However other forms of editing, such as insert, are missing. Let's take a look at the `Read` and `Readln` standard procedures.

The `Read` and `Readln` procedures can be set to recognize several logical devices. These include:

CON :   Console. Input from the keyboard is temporarily stored in a buffer. In this mode, the input can be edited with the backspace and Ctrl-X.

TRM :   Terminal. The input from the keyboard is unbuffered.

KBD :   Keyboard. No echo is sent to the screen during keyboard input. The characters entered are invisible.

Since CON, TRM and KBD are predefined as text files, they are quite easy to use. When using `Read` or `Readln` to read from the keyboard, the procedure call looks as follows:

Readln(CON,param);

The call is identical for TRM and KBD.

If device CON is used, it may be omitted from the call, since it is the default device:

Readln(param);   equivalent to Readln(CON,param);

This default device setting can be changed by using the **B** compiler directive. With **$B-** the input file TRM is set as the default, meaning that every read operation without explicit specification of the text file is made from the terminal (unbuffered).

The KBD text file has one very important practical use. Here is an example:

```
program keyboard;
var
   ch : char;
begin
   read(KBD,ch);
   write(ch);
end.
```

This program waits for a keypress, stores the value of the key in variable ch and displays the character on the screen.

The main point here is that the input does not need to be ended with the RETURN key. This feature can be put to good use in menu selections or other types of input routines. The Input function, described later, uses this technique.

Sometimes it's necessary to limit the length of the input line in order to maintain a defined input field. This can be done in Turbo Pascal by changing the predefined variable buflen.

Normally this variable contains the value 127, which sets the maximum number of characters per input line to 127. This value can be changed within your program in order to define a smaller input field. A line length greater than127 characters is not allowed.

Note: You must set the contents of buflen immediately before using the Read or Readln procedures because Turbo Pascal resets buflen to 127 after the Read or Readln.

```
program fieldtest;
var
     st : string[10];
begin
   Write('Field 1:');
   buflen := 10;
   Readln(st);
   Write('Field 2:');
   buflen := 5;
   Readln(st);
```

```
   Write('Field 3:');
   buflen := 1;
   Readln(st);
end.
```

5.1 Function description

Input is a function which makes it easy to enter characters. The following editing functions are available:

CP/M	MS-DOS	Effect
Ctrl-S	<-	The cursor is moved one position to the left without deleting a character. The input function is ended when the left field boundary is reached.
Ctrl-D	->	As above, but moves to the right.
Ctrl-G	DEL	The character to the left of the cursor is deleted and all characters to the right of the cursor are moved one position to the left.
Ctrl-V	INS	A blank is inserted at the current cursor position and the right portion of the input field is moved one position to the right. When the input field is full, this operation is not allowed so that no characters will be lost.

In addition to these keys, several other are check to determine if input has ended.

Input is a function that returns a value indicating the key with which the function was exited. The value is of type byte. Knowing which key was pressed can be used to initiate certain actions (such as determining the next input position based on which cursor control key was pressed).

The following table contains the key function values:

CP/M	MS-DOS	Function value	
RETURN	RETURN	0	
Ctrl-S	←	1	
Ctrl-D	→	2	
Ctrl-E	↑	3	
Ctrl-X	↓	4	
Ctrl-W	HOME	5	
	PageUP	6	only MS-DOS
	PageDown	7	only MS-DOS

Input is called with the following parameters:

Parameters for CP/M Version:

par1,par2 :   XY position of the input field.
In the CP/M version the position must be specified explicitly because the current cursor position cannot be determined.

par3 :   Length of the input field.

par4 :   Set of valid input characters.
The set must be defined as set of char;

par5 :   a string variable to contain the inputted data after the function is exited. The length of the string variable must be as large as the field size. If this variable is initialized with a string before the function is called, it will appear in the input field. This makes it possible to set defaults for input fields.

Parameters for MS-DOS Version:

par1 :   sets whether or not the characters will be echoed on the screen. The same attribute numbers are used exactly as for the procedure `Print`.

par2 :   Length of the input field.

par3 :   Same as par4 of the CP/M version.

par4 :   Same as par5 of the CP/M version.

We'll demonstrate the use of the `Input` function in the following two examples (one for CP/M and one for MS-DOS).

Test program for CP/M:

```pascal
program testinput;
   type
   Cset = set of char;
   var
   line : byte;
   column : byte;
   leng : byte;
   Ctype : Cset;
   buffer : string[80];
   status : byte;

{$I input.fnc}

begin
   line := 20;
   column := 30;
   leng := 30;
   buffer := 'this is the default field';
   Ctype := ['A'..'Z', 'a'..'z'];

   status := input(column, line, leng, Ctype,
buffer);
end.
```

Test program for MS-DOS:

```pascal
program testinput;

  type
    Cset = set of char;

  var
    line : byte;
    column : byte;
    leng : byte;
    Ctype : Cset;
    atr : byte;
    buffer : string[80];
    status : byte;

{$I wpage.fnc}
{$I page.prc}
{$I wheresx.fnc}
{$I wheresy.fnc}
{$I gotosxy.prc}
{$I print.prc}
{$I input.fnc}

begin
  line := 20;
  column := 30;
  leng := 30;
  buffer := 'this is the default field';
  Ctype := ['A'..'Z', 'a'..'z'];
  atr := 9;

  gotoxy(column, line);

  status := input(atr, leng, Ctype, buffer);
end.
```

5.2 *Input* - listing for CP/M:

Save on disk under the name **input.fnc**

```
1     function Input (x, y, l : byte;
2                       var tp, bf) : byte;
3
4       const
5         Del = ^G;
6         Ins = ^V;
7         CLeft = ^S;
8         CRight = ^D;
9         CUp = ^E;
10        CDown = ^X;
11        CHome = ^W;
12
13      type
14        ascii = set of char;
15
16      var
17        ch : char;
18        pos : byte;
19        buffer : string[80];
20        flag : byte;
21        t : ascii;
22
23    begin
24
25      move(tp, t, SizeOf(tp));
26
27      move(bf, buffer, mem[addr(bf)] + 1);
28
29
30      gotoxy(x, y);
31      write(buffer);
32      gotoxy(x, y);
33
34      flag := 0;
35      pos := 1;
36
37
```

```
38        repeat
39          read(kbd, ch);
40
41          case ch of
42
43
44            Del :
45              if pos > 1 then
46                begin
47                  pos := pos - 1;
48                  delete(buffer, pos, 1);
49                  gotoxy(x, y);
50                  write(buffer);
51                  write(' ');
52                  gotoxy(x + pos - 1, y);
53                end;
54
55            Ins :
56              if length(buffer) < 1 then
57                begin
58                  insert(' ', buffer, pos);
59                  gotoxy(x, y);
60                  write(buffer);
61                  gotoxy(x + pos - 1, y);
62                end;
63
64            CLeft :
65              if pos > 1 then
66                begin
67                  pos := pos - 1;
68                  gotoxy(x + pos - 1, y);
69                end
70              else
71                flag := 1;
72
73            CRight :
74              if pos < length(buffer) then
75                begin
76                  pos := pos + 1;
77                  gotoxy(x + pos - 1, y);
78                end
79              else
80                flag := 2;
81
```

```
82              Cup :
83                 flag := 3;
84              CDown :
85                 flag := 4;
86              CHome :
87                 flag := 5;
88
89              otherwise
90                 if (pos < 1) and (ch <> chr(13)) and
                      (ch <> chr(8)) and (ch in t) then
91                    begin
92                       delete(buffer, pos, 1);
93                       insert(ch, buffer, pos);
94                       write(ch);
95                       pos := pos + 1;
96                    end;
97           end;
98
99        until (ch = chr(13)) or (flag <> 0);
100
101       move(buffer, bf, length(buffer) + 1);
102
103       input := flag;
104
105    end;
```

5.3 *Input* - listing for MS-DOS:

Save to disk under the name **input.fnc**

```
1    function input (m, l : byte;
2                         var tp, bf) : byte;
3
4       const
5         Del = 'S';
6         Ins = 'R';
7         CLeft = 'K';
8         CRight = 'M';
9         CUp = 'H';
10        CDown = 'P';
11        CHome = 'G';
12        PUp = 'I';
13        PDown = 'Q';
14
15      type
16        ascii = set of char;
17
18      var
19        x, y, p : byte;
20        ch : char;
21        c : string[1];
22        pos : byte;
23        sg, os : integer;
24        buffer : string[80];
25        flag : byte;
26        t : ascii;
27
28   begin
29
30      sg := seg(tp);
31      os := ofs(tp);
32      move(tp, t, 32);
33
34      sg := seg(bf);
35      os := ofs(bf);
36      move(bf, buffer, mem[sg : os] + 1);
37      p := wpage;
38      x := wheresx(p);
39      y := wheresy(p);
40
```

```
41        print(p, m, buffer);
42        gotosxy(p, x, y);
43
44        flag := 0;
45        pos := 1;
46
47        repeat
48          read(kbd, ch);
49          if ch = chr(27) then
50            begin
51              read(kbd, ch);
52              case ch of
53
54                Del :
55                  if pos > 1 then
56                    begin
57                      c := ' ';
58                      pos := pos - 1;
59                      delete(buffer, pos, 1);
60                      gotosxy(p, x, y);
61                      print(p, m, buffer);
62                      print(p, m, c);
63                      gotosxy(p, x + pos - 1, y);
64                    end;
65
66                Ins :
67                  if length(buffer) < 1 then
68                    begin
69                      c := ' ';
70                      insert(c, buffer, pos);
71                      gotosxy(p, x, y);
72                      print(p, m, buffer);
73                      gotosxy(p, x + pos - 1, y);
74                    end;
75
76                CLeft :
77                  if pos > 1 then
78                    begin
79                      pos := pos - 1;
80                      gotosxy(p, x + pos - 1, y);
81                    end
82                  else
83                    flag := 1;
84
```

```
 85                    CRight :
 86                      if pos < length(buffer) then
 87                        begin
 88                          pos := pos + 1;
 89                          gotosxy(p, x + pos - 1, y);
 90                        end
 91                      else
 92                        flag := 2;
 93
 94                    CUp :
 95                      flag := 3;
 96                    CDown :
 97                      flag := 4;
 98                    CHome :
 99                      flag := 5;
100                    PUp :
101                      flag := 6;
102                    PDown :
103                      flag := 7;
104
105               end;
106
107             end
108           else if (pos < l + 1) and (ch <>
                        chr(13)) and (ch <> chr(8)) then
109             begin
110               if ch in t then
111                 begin
112                   c := ch;
113                   delete(buffer, pos, 1);
114                   insert(ch, buffer, pos);
115                   print(p, m, c);
116                   pos := pos + 1;
117                 end;
118             end;
119       until (ch = chr(13)) or (flag <> 0);
120
121       move(buffer, bf, length(buffer) + 1);
122       input := flag;
123     end;
```

5.4 Program description

In this description we'll limit ourselves to the MS-DOS version since it is more complex than the CP/M version.

In lines 30 to 32 the third function parameter `tp` is copied to `t` using the procedure `Move`. This procedure prevents a type definition from being bound with a specific identifier in the calling program.

The contents of `bf` are moved to buffer in lines 34 to 36 using procedure `Move` again. The address of the variables is previously placed into variables `sg` (segment) and `os` (offset).

In lines 37 to 39 the current page and the X-position and Y-position of the cursor are assigned to the variables `p`, `x`, and `y`. In line 44 the variable `flag` is initialized to zero. It will eventually contain the code for the escape key.

The variable `pos`, which contains the current cursor position in the input field, is initialized to one in order to define the starting position of the cursor in the input field (line 45).

In line 48 the keyboard is read without the echo appearing on the screen, and the result is assigned to the variable `ch`. The value in `ch` is checked for ESC (escape value chr(27)). The control keys on the IBM PC, (e.g. cursor control keys), are indicated as an escape sequence consisting of the escape character (ESC) and a character following it. If an escape character is recognized, the keyboard is read again in order to get the second character of this escape sequence (line 51).

In CP/M, control characters are represented as single values. Therefore there is no equivalent escape character sequence.

The delete function is performed in lines 54 to 63. A check is made to see if the cursor position is greater than 1. If so, there is no data to delete. If the cursor position is greater than 1, the delete function can be performed. The cursor position in `pos` is decremented by one and a character is removed from the buffer using the standard procedure `Delete`. In lines 59 to 62 the new contents of buffer are written to the screen and the character beneath the cursor is overwritten with a space. The cursor position is set in line 63.

When the INS key is pressed, lines 66 through 74 of the case-statement are processed. In line 65 a check is made to see if the number of characters in buffer is less than the maximum field length. This prevents part of the input field from being moved past the field boundaries during insertion. A space is inserted at the current cursor position using the standard procedure Insert and the contents of buffer are written to the screen. The cursor position is set in line 73.

In lines 76 to 83, the cursor is moved to the left. If the cursor position in the input field is already 1, the variable flag is assigned the value 1 and the cursor is not moved.

In lines 85 to 92, the cursor is moved to the right. If the cursor position in the input field has already reached the last field position, the variable flag is assigned the value 2 and the cursor is not moved.

The remaining control characters are handled in lines 94 through 103.

In line 108 a check is made to see if the character entered was CR or backspace or if the field length was exceeded. In this case the character is not accepted into buffer.

A check is made in line 110 to see if the character entered is in the set of allowable characters. In the case that the character is allowed, it is inserted into buffer at the current field position (a character already present there is overwritten) and the cursor is moved one position to the right.

The **repeat**-loop is terminated when the characters entered is equal to CR or when flag is not equal to zero. In this case the contents of buffer are copied to bf and flag is assigned to the function variable Input.

5.5 *ClrKbd* procedure

Procedure ClrKbd clears the keyboard buffer. This can be very useful if you use certain DOS functions for character input which do not clear the keyboard buffer themselves.

Save to disk under the name **clrkbd.prc**

```
1    procedure ClrKbd;
2
3    type regtype = record
4                     ax,bx,cx,dx,bp,
5                     di,si,ds,es,flags : integer;
6                   end;
7
8    var register : regtype;
9        ah,al    : byte;
10
11   begin
12
13     ah := $0C;
14
15     with register do
16       begin
17         ax := ah shl 8;
18         MsDos(register);
19       end;
20   end;
```

ClrKbd uses MS-DOS function 12 (hex 0C), which is loaded into the high-order byte of the ax register (line 17). After this, the MsDos procedure is called.

CHAPTER 6

Chapter 6: *Mask* - A mask generator program

6.1 Function description

Easy-to-use input and output of data is a goal of every programmer. Using *screen masks* is one approach to reaching this goal.

This section is concerned with a general solution to creating these screen masks. A screen mask (we'll refer to it simply as a mask) is a description of the data and the fields that may be entered on a single screen. We can automate the definition of these masks by using a mask generator.

The mask generator consists of two parts:

   1. Mask Editor
   2. Mask Interpreter

For simplicity, we'll use the Turbo Pascal editor as the Mask Editor.

A mask is designed in exactly the same form as it is to later appear on the screen. A screen format of 25 rows by 80 columns is used.

Individual input fields are marked with special characters. When the mask interpreter sees such a special character, it recognizes it as a specific type of input field.

Several field types are allowed. They vary according to the version of Turbo that you're using. The following field types can be specified:

in CP/M:

   #   : numerical input field
   @ : alphanumeric input field

in MS-DOS:

This version has four times as many types of input fields:

Numerical fields	Alphanumeric fields
% : attrib = 1	! : attrib = 1
^ : attrib = 3	# : attrib = 3
& : attrib = 6	@ : attrib = 6
* : attrib = 7	$: attrib = 7

The attribute numbers are identical to those used in procedure `print` (Section 4.3.1).

In this example, eight input fields are defined using the Turbo Pascal editor (MS-DOS version):

```
field 1 :!!!!!!!!!  field 5 :%%%%%%%%%%  field 7 :&&&&&&&&&&&&

field 2 :@@@@@@@@  field 6 :^^^^^^^^^^

field 3 :########                field 8 :************

field 4 :$$$$$$$$
```

The following control keys can be used during input:

CP/M	MS-DOS	Purpose
Ctrl-S	←	The cursor is moved one position to the left without deleting a character. When the left border of the input field or the last character entered is reached, the field is exited and the cursor is placed in the neighboring field to the left. If there is no field to the left, the cursor moves to the rightmost field of the previous line.
Ctrl-D	→	As above, except the cursor moves to the right. If the field is exited and there are no fields to the right, the cursor moves to the leftmost field of the next line.

Ctrl-E	↑	The cursor moves to the input field on the line above the current one.
Ctrl-X	↓	The cursor moves to the input field on the line below the current one.
Ctrl-W	HOME	The cursor is placed in the first input field on the screen.
Ctrl-G	DEL	
Ctrl-V	INS	same as procedure *Input* (from Chapter 5)
	PageUp	By using these keys the user can switch between individual screen masks. This option is
	PageDown	available only in the MS-DOS version.

The mask generator consists of two procedures: `mask` and `scan` which you can merge into your programs.

`Maskgen` is a small test program to show you how the type declarations for the two procedures `mask` and `scan` are made.

6.1.1 *Maskgen* - listing for CP/M

```
 1    program Maskgen;
 2
 3      type
 4        fieldnum = 1..100;
 5
 6        element = record
 7            line : byte;
 8            column : byte;
 9            len : byte;
10            Ctype : set of char;
11          end;
12
13        str80 = string[80];
14        str12 = string[12];
```

```
15          vrstr = array[fieldnum] of str80;
16          arlem = array[fieldnum] of element;
17
18          parrec = record
19               field : arlem;
20               name : str12;
21               max : byte;
22               fnr : byte;
23             end;
24
25        var
26           jf : byte;
27           mpar : parrec;
28           mstr : vrstr;
29
30    {$I open_r.fnc}
31
32    {$I input.fnc}
33
34    {$I mask.fnc}
35
36    {$I scan.prc}
37
38      procedure inp;
39
40      begin
41        clrscr;
42        with mpar do
43          begin
44            write('Mask name : ');
45            readln(name);
46            fnr := 1;
47          end;
48      end;
49
50    begin
51
52      repeat
53        inp;
54        clrscr;
55      until mask(mpar);
56
57      for jf := 1 to mpar.max do
58        mstr[jf] := ' demo ';
```

```
59
60      scan(mstr, mpar);
61
62      clrscr;
63      for jf := 1 to mpar.max do
64        writeln(mstr[jf]);
65    end.
```

6.1.2 *Maskgen* - listing for MS-DOS

```
 1    program Maskgen;
 2
 3      type
 4        screen = 0..3;
 5        fieldnum = 1..100;
 6
 7        element = record
 8            line : byte;
 9            column : byte;
10            len : byte;
11            Ctype : set of char;
12            atr : byte;
13          end;
14
15        str80 = string[80];
16        str12 = string[12];
17        vrstr = array[fieldnum] of str80;
18        arlem = array[fieldnum] of element;
19
20        parrec = record
21            field : arlem;
22            name : str12;
23            max : byte;
24            fnr : byte;
25          end;
26
27        arpar = array[screen] of parrec;
28        arstr = array[screen] of vrstr;
29
30      var
31        maxscr : byte;
32        l1, l2 : byte;
33        mpar : arpar;
34        mstr : arstr;
35
36    {$I open_r.fnc}
37    {$I wpage..fnc}
38    {$I page.prc}
39    {$I wheresx.fnc}
40    {$I wheresy.fnc}
```

```
41    {$I gotosxy.prc}
42    {$I print.prc}
43    {$I input.fnc}
44
45    {$I mask.fnc}
46    {$I scan.prc}
47
48      procedure inp;
49                    •
50        var
51          lf : byte;
52
53      begin
54        clrscr;
55        write('Number of masks : ');
56        readln(maxscr);
57
58        for lf := 0 to maxscr - 1 do
59          begin
60            with mpar[lf] do
61              begin
62                write('Mask ', lf, ' : ');
63                readln(name);
64                fnr := 1;
65              end;
66          end;
67        clrscr;
68      end;
69
70    begin
71
72      repeat
73        inp
74      until mask(mpar, maxscr);
75
76      for l1 := 0 to maxscr - 1 do
77        for l2 := 1 to mpar[l1].max do
78          mstr[l1, l2] := ' demo ';
79
80      scan(mstr, mpar, maxscr);
81
```

```
82        page(0);
83        clrscr;
84
85        for l1 := 0 to maxscr - 1 do
86          for l2 := 1 to mpar[l1].max do
87            writeln(mstr[l1, l2]);
88      end.
```

6.1.3 More details about masks

The parameters representing the individual fields of the screen are stored in a variable of type element. The record components line, column, len, Ctype and atr determine the field's position on the screen, its length, the set of allowable characters, and the display attributes for the procedure Print.

These are placed into an array of element in the type arlem in order to be able to address a variable of all fields of the mask.

The specifications of the mask are placed in a variable of type parrec which is made up of the following components:

Field: is of type arlem and contains the field parameters of the field.

Name: contains the mask name.

Max: contains the number of fields.

Fnr: is the number of the field which should be edited first.

Function mask has the task of reading in the mask definition created by the editor, displaying it, and determining the field attributes. This done as follows:

The programmer passes a variable of type parrec containing the mask name and the number of the field to be edited first and calls function mask. If the mask definition is found, it is built on the screen and the function value is set to true. Otherwise the mask definition was not found on the disk.

If the mask definition was found, then the variable of type parrec contains all of the specifications of the mask as described above.

In a program it would look like this:

```
var param : parrec;
begin
  param.name:='maskname';
  param.fnr :=1;

  if mask(param) then
     write('mask found')
  else
     write('mask not found');
end.
```

In the MS-DOS version, multiple masks (up to four) may be built with one call to mask. This is the reason the mask specifications are placed in an array of parrec and the variable which contains them is of type arpar.

Function mask then returns the boolean value true if the procedure could read all of the masks. Otherwise only the masks which were found are constructed and function mask returns the value false.

The masks are built from the last page to the first page. If you want to read three masks, the first mask is built on page 2, the second on page 1, and the last mask on page 0.

In addition to the mask name, you must also pass the number of masks to function mask.

For example:

```
var param : arpar;
    maxscr:byte;
begin
  maxscr:=2;
  param[0].name:='mask name';
  param[1].name:='mask name';
```

```
    param[2].name:='mask name';
    if mask(param,maxscr) then
       write('all masks found')
    else
       write('not all masks found');
  end.
```

The index of the variable param determines the page number.

Procedure Scan requires a variable of type parrec defined by mask (arpar in the MS-DOS version) and a variable of type vrstr (arstr in the MS-DOS version) to which the field contents are assigned. The number of the mask must also be passed in the MS-DOS version.

Scan allows the user to edit the fields of the mask (or masks in the MS-DOS version) by passing the field parameters to the function Input and reacting to its result accordingly.

It is exited when the RETURN key is pressed, after which the field contents can be found in the various components of the variable of type vrstr (or arstr).

The variable to which the field contents are assigned should be initialized before calling the procedure scan. Scan and Input do not do this. In the example program we initialized all of the fields with the string constants demo. When the fields are first displayed on the screen no check is made to see if the characters are in the valid range or if the maximum field length is exceeded.

As you can see from the listing of the function mask, we have limited ourselves to just two field types in the CP/M version. This can be changed by the user.

The number of field types is determined by the declaration

```
    type son = array [1..n]
```

The field markers are defined as constants

```
    const sc : son = ('#','@',..,charn);
```

The assignment of the set of allowable characters to the component Ctype of the variable Field is done in the **case** statement:

```
with field do
  begin
    case sa of
       1 : Ctype := type1;
       2 : Ctype := type2;


              .
              .
              .

       n : Ctype := typen;
    end;
  end;
```

The set variables (or constants) must be previously defined. For example:

```
var typen : set of char;
begin
  typen:=['0'..'9'];
```

or

```
Type ascii = set of char;

Const typen : ascii=['0'..'9'];
```

In the MS-DOS version, we combined the field type with the field attribute, requiring a large number of field markers but simplifying the creation of the masks.

Components `Ctype` and `atr` of the variable `Field` are determined in the **case** statement:

```
case sa of
  1 : begin Ctype:=type1; atr:=attribute1; end;
    :
    :
  n : begin Ctype:=typen; atr:=attributen; end;
end;
```

6.1.4 *Open_R* function

The following function Open_r is a component of all programs that access disk files and is an include file. It opens a file for reading and takes over the error handling.

Save to disk under the name **open_r.fnc**

```
1    function open_r (var a : text;
2                     var dt) : boolean;
3
4      var
5        d : string[12];
6
7    begin
8    move(dt,d,mem[seg(dt):ofs(dt)]+1);
9    {move(dt,d,mem[addr(dt)]+1); CPM only}
10   {$i-}
11     assign(a, d);
12     reset(a);
13     if IOresult <> 0 then
14       begin
15         close(a);
16         open_r := false;
17       end
18     else
19       open_r := true;
20   {$I+}
21   end;
```

6.2 *Mask* - mask interpreter listing for CP/M

Save to disk as **mask.fnc**

```
1    function Mask (var prm : parrec) : boolean;
2
3      type
4        ascii = set of char;
5
6      const
7        numr : ascii = ['0'..'9','+','-',' '];
8        alfa : ascii = ['a'..'z','A'..'Z',' '];
9
10     var
11       maskf : text;
12
13     procedure construct (var source : text);
14
15       type
16         son = array[1..2] of char;
17
18       const sc : son = ('#','@');
19
20       var
21         lin : string[80];
22         cl, ln : byte;
23         mx, sa : byte;
24
25     begin
26       with prm do
27         begin
28           max := 0;
29           ln := 1;
30           gotoxy(1, 1);
31           while not eof(source) do
32             begin
33               readln(source, lin);
34               for sa := 1 to 2 do
35                 begin
36                   while pos(sc[sa], lin) <> 0
                      do
37                     begin
38                       max := max + 1;
```

```
39                          with field[max] do
40                            begin
41                              column := pos(sc[sa],
                                   lin);
42                              line := ln;
43                              len := 0;
44
45                              case sa of
46                                1 :
47                                  Ctype := numr;
48                                2 :
49                                  Ctype := alfa +
                                           numr;
50                              end;
51
52                              repeat
53                                lin[pos(sc[sa],
                                     lin)] := ' ';
54                                len := len + 1;
55                              until lin[column +
                                   len] <> sc[sa];
56                            end;
57                          end;
58                      end;
59                    writeln(lin);
60                    ln := ln + 1;
61                end;
62            end;
63      end;
64
65    begin
66      if open_r(maskf, prm.name) then
67        begin
68          construct(maskf);
69          close(maskf);
70          mask := true;
71        end
72      else
73        mask := false;
74    end;
```

Save to disk under the name **scan.prc**

```
1    procedure scan (var buf : vrstr;
2                     prm : parrec);
3
4      var
5        ln, l : byte;
6        cl, li : byte;
7        tp : set of char;
8        flag : boolean;
9
10     procedure pos (fd : byte);
11     begin
12       with prm.field[fd] do
13         begin
14           cl := column;
15           li := line;
16           tp := Ctype;
17           ln := len;
18           gotoxy(cl, li);
19         end;
20     end;
21
22     procedure find (i : byte, var d : byte);
23       var
24         dif1, dif2 : byte;
25         gf : boolean;
26
27     begin
28       gf := false;
29       with prm do
30         begin
31           while (d < max) and not gf and
         (field[d].line = field[succ(d)].line) do
32             begin
33               dif1 := abs(field[d].column -
                          field[i].column);
34               dif2 := abs(field[succ(d)].column
                          - field[i].column);
35               if dif1 < dif2 then
36                 gf := true
37               else
38                 d := succ(d);
39             end;
```

```
40          end;
41       end;
42
43       procedure down (var i : byte);
44         var
45            d : byte;
46            g : boolean;
47       begin
48         d := i;
49         g := false;
50         with prm do
51           begin
52             while (d < max) and not g do
53               begin
54                 if field[d].line =
                      field[succ(d)].line then
55                   d := succ(d)
56                 else
57                   begin
58                     d := succ(d);
59                     g := true;
60                     find(i, d);
61                     i := d;
62                   end;
63               end;
64           end;
65       end;
66
67       procedure up (var i : byte);
68         var
69            d : byte;
70            g : boolean;
71       begin
72         d := i;
73         g := false;
74         with prm do
75           begin
76             while (d > 1) and not g do
77               begin
78                 if field[d].line =
                      field[pred(d)].line then
79                   d := pred(d)
80                 else
81                   begin
```

```
82                    d := pred(d);
83                    while (d > 1) and
        (field[d].line = field[pred(d)].line) do
84                      begin
85                        d := pred(d);
86                      end;
87                    g := true;
88                    find(i, d);
89                    i := d;
90                  end;
91              end;
92          end;
93     end;
94
95     procedure left (var i : byte);
96     begin
97       if i > 1 then
98         i := pred(i);
99     end;
100
101    procedure right (var i : byte);
102    begin
103      if i < prm.max then
104        i := succ(i);
105    end;
106
107  begin
108    flag := false;
109
110    with prm do
111      begin
112        for l := 1 to max do
113          begin
114            pos(l);
115            write(buf[l]);
116          end;
117      end;
118
119    repeat
120      with prm do
121        begin
122          pos(fnr);
123
```

```
124          case input(cl, li, ln, tp, buf[fnr])
               of
125          0 :
126             flag := true;
127          1 :
128             left(fnr);
129          2 :
130             right(fnr);
131          3 :
132             up(fnr);
133          4 :
134             down(fnr);
135          5 :
136             fnr := 1;
137          end;
138        end;
139     until flag;
140   end;
```

6.3 *Mask* - mask interpreter listing for MS-DOS

Save to disk as **mask.fnc**

```
1      function Mask (var prm : arpar;
2                        maxscr : byte) : boolean;
3
4        type
5          ascii = set of char;
6
7        const numr:ascii =['0'..'9','+','-',' '];
8              alfa:ascii =['a'..'z','A'..'Z',' '];
9
10       var
11         maskf : text;
12         scr : byte;
13
14       procedure construct (var source : text;
15                           s : byte);
16
17         type
18           son = array[1..8] of char;
19
20         const sc : son = ('!','#','@','$',
                             '%','^','&','*');
21
22         var
23           lin : str80;
24           cl, li : byte;
25           mx, sa : byte;
26
27       begin
28         with prm[s] do
29           begin
30             max := 0;
31             li := 0;
32             gotosxy(s, 0, 0);
33             while not eof(source) do
34               begin
35                 readln(source, lin);
36                 for sa := 1 to 8 do
```

137

```
37          begin
38            while pos(sc[sa], lin) <> 0
                do
39            begin
40              max := max + 1;
41              with field[max] do
42                begin
43                  column := pos(sc[sa],
                              lin) - 1;
44                  line := li;
45                  len := 0;

47                  case sa of
48                    1 :
49                      begin
50                        atr := 1;
51                        Ctype := alfa +
                                numr
52                      end;
53                    2 :
54                      begin
55                        atr := 3;
56                        Ctype := alfa +
                                numr
57                      end;
58                    3 :
59                      begin
60                        atr := 7;
61                        Ctype := alfa +
                                numr
62                      end;
63                    4 :
64                      begin
65                        atr := 11;
66                        Ctype := alfa +
                                numr
67                      end;
68                    5 :
69                      begin
70                        atr := 1;
71                        Ctype := alfa
72                      end;
```

```
73                                  6 :
74                                    begin
75                                      atr := 3;
76                                      Ctype := alfa
77                                    end;
78                                  7 :
79                                    begin
80                                      atr := 7;
81                                      Ctype := alfa
82                                    end;
83                                  8 :
84                                    begin
85                                      atr := 11;
86                                      Ctype := alfa
87                                    end;
88                                end;
89
90                                repeat
91                                  lin[pos(sc[sa],
                                        lin)] := ' ';
92                                  len := len + 1;
93                                until lin[column + 1
                                      + len] <> sc[sa];
94                              end;
95                            end;
96                          end;
97                        print(s, 1, line);
98                        li := li + 1;
99                        gotosxy(s, 0, wheresy(s) + 1);
100                     end;
101                 end;
102           end;
103
104     begin
105       mask := true;
106       scr := maxscr;
107       if (maxscr > 0) and (maxscr < 4) then
108         begin
109           while (scr > 0) do
110             begin
111               if open_r(maskf, prm[scr - 1].name)
                    then
```

```
112                    begin
113                       construct(maskf, scr - 1);
114                       close(maskf);
115                    end
116                  else
117                    mask := false;
118                  scr := scr - 1;
119               end;
120            end
121          else
122            mask := false;
123       end;
```

Save to disk under the name **scan.prc**

```
1     procedure scan (var buf : arstr;
2                      prm : arpar;
3                      maxscr : byte);
4
5        var
6           scr, ll : byte;
7           at, ln : byte;
8           tp : set of char;
9           flag : boolean;
10
11       procedure pos (f : byte);
12       begin
13          with prm[scr].field[f] do
14             begin
15                gotosxy(scr, column, line);
16                at := atr;
17                tp := Ctype;
18                ln := len;
19             end;
20       end;
21
22       procedure find (i : byte, var d : byte);
23          var
24             dif1, dif2 : byte;
25             gf : boolean;
26
```

```
27      begin
28         gf := false;
29         with prm[scr] do
30           begin
31             while (d < max) and not gf and
            (field[d].line = field[succ(d)].line) do
32                 begin
33                     dif1 := abs(field[d].column -
                            field[i].column);
34                     dif2 := abs(field[succ(d)].column
                            - field[i].column);
35                     if dif1 < dif2 then
36                       gf := true
37                     else
38                       d := succ(d);
39                 end;
40           end;
41      end;
42
43      procedure down (var i : byte);
44         var
45            d : byte;
46            g : boolean;
47      begin
48         d := i;
49         g := false;
50         with prm[scr] do
51           begin
52             while (d < max) and not g do
53                 begin
54                     if field[d].line =
                        field[succ(d)].line then
55                       d := succ(d)
56                     else
57                       begin
58                         d := succ(d);
59                         g := true;
60                         find(i, d);
61                         i := d;
62                       end;
63                 end;
64           end;
65      end;
66
```

```
67        procedure up (var i : byte);
68          var
69            d : byte;
70            g : boolean;
71        begin
72          d := i;
73          g := false;
74          with prm[scr] do
75            begin
76              while (d > 1) and not g do
77                begin
78                  if field[d].line =
                       field[pred(d)].line then
79                    d := pred(d)
80                  else
81                    begin
82                      d := pred(d);
83                      while (d > 1) and
            (field[d].line = field[pred(d)].line) do
84                        begin
85                          d := pred(d);
86                        end;
87                      g := true;
88                      find(i, d);
89                      i := d;
90                    end;
91                end;
92            end;
93        end;
94
95        procedure left (var i : byte);
96        begin
97          if i > 1 then
98            i := pred(i);
99        end;
100
101       procedure right (var i : byte);
102       begin
103         if i < prm[scr].max then
104           i := succ(i);
105       end;
106
```

```
107    begin
108       maxscr := maxscr - 1;
109
110       for scr := 0 to maxscr do
111         begin
112           with prm[scr] do
113             begin
114               for ll := 1 to max do
115                 begin
116                   with field[ll] do
117                     begin
118                       gotosxy(scr, column, line);
119                       print(scr, atr, buf[scr,
                                 ll]);
120                     end;
121                 end;
122             end;
123         end;
124
125       scr := 0;
126       flag := false;
127
128       repeat
129         page(scr);
130         with prm[scr] do
131           begin
132             pos(fnr);
133
134             case input(at,ln,tp,buf[scr,fnr]) of
135               0 :
136                 flag := true;
137               1 :
138                 left(fnr);
139               2 :
140                 right(fnr);
141               3 :
142                 up(fnr);
143               4 :
144                 down(fnr);
145               5 :
146                 fnr := 1;
147               6 :
148                 if scr < maxscr then
149                   scr := scr + 1;
```

```
150                 7 :
151                     if scr > 0 then
152                         scr := scr - 1;
153                 end;
154             end;
155         until flag;
156     end;
```

6.4 Program description

The list of formal parameters for the function mask has already been explained for both versions, so we can now proceed to the program description.

All line numbers in the following description refer to the listing of the CP/M version. The corresponding lines in the MS-DOS version are easy to find.

The type declaration ascii in line 4 serves only to define the constants numr and alfa which determine the sets of legal input characters.

In the **if** statement in line 66, a determination is made to see if the file prm.name can be opened for reading. If it can, procedure construct is called. If open_r returns the value false, however, the mask definition is not on the disk and the function mask is exited with the value false.

In lines 15-18 of the procedure construct, the field types and field markers are set. The mask definition is then read, line by line (line 33) and the lines are searched for field markers in the **for**-loop (line 34).

In line 36, pos is used to determine if a field marker is present in the line. If so, the number of fields in max is incremented by 1 in line 38. The position of the field marker in the line, the line number in variable li, and the field length are passed corresponding to the components of the variable field, in which the length is first initialized to zero.

The component Ctype for the field marker is set in the CASE instruction (lines 45-52). In the **repeat**-loop following it (line 52-55) the field markers are removed from the line and the field length is incremented. This is done until a different character is found in the next column.

If the condition in line 36 is fulfilled, the whole procedure is repeated. Otherwise variable `sa` is incremented by one in the for-loop. The search starts over from the beginning and is continued until `sa` has run through all of the field markers defined in variable `sc`. After this is done, the line is printed (59-60) and the line number is incremented by one. The whole thing is repeated until `eof(maskf)` is reached.

The MS-DOS version needs no special treatment since the differences are limited to the system-dependent character output and the formal parameters.

The procedure `construct` is here called in a **while**-loop (109-120) for each mask, in which `mask` is set to `false` if a mask definition is not found. In line 106 the variable `scr` which corresponds to the page number is set to the number of the mask and then decremented in line 118, which has the result that the masks are constructed from the highest page number to page 0. The construction is carried out until variable `scr` reaches zero, even when a mask definition could not be read in the mean time.

In the explanation of the procedure `scan` we will limit ourselves to the MS-DOS version.

As we have already indicated, the selectable screen pages in MS-DOS are numbered from 0 on up. The parameter passed to `scan` in `maxscr` gives the number of masks which is one greater than the number of the last mask. This is why the value in `maxscr` is corrected in line 118.

Next the contents of the various fields are displayed in lines 110-123. The variable `scr` which specifies the number of the current page is et to zero in line 125. This means that the input begins with page zero.

The boolean variable `flag`, which serves as a flag for the **repeat**-loop in lines 128-155, is initialized to `false` in line 126.

In line 129 the screen is switched to the screen page given in scr. The procedure `pos` is called with `prm[scr]` in lne 132. This procedure transfers the components of the variable `field` and passes them to `input`.

The values returned from `input` function as follows:

0   RETURN key
     `flag` is set to `false`, which fulfills the condition for the **repeat**-loop and causes the procedure `scan` to be exited.

1   ← key
     Procedure left decrements the field number if fnr>0.

2   → key
     Procedure right increments the field numer if fnr<max
     (number of fields).

3   ↑ key
     Procedure up searches for the last field in the previous line and
     calls procedure find. The procedure find searches in the line
     just found for a field whose starting column has the smallest
     difference to the column of the current field. If no field with a
     smaller line number is found, the cursor remains in the current
     field.

4   ↓ key
     Procedure down searches for the first field whose line number is
     greater than that of the current field, and continues as with the
     procedure up.

5   HOME key
     The current field number is set to 1.

6   PageUp key
     The current page number is incremented if scr is less than the
     maximum page number.

7   PageDown key
     The current page number is decremented if scr>0.

As you see, only the variable scr or fnr is affected in the various
case branches. The actual positioning is done in line 132. If input is now
called with new values, the cursor appears in the field defined by them.

CHAPTER 7

Chapter 7: Turbo Pascal and Disk Management

7.1 *Catalog* procedure for CP/M

The program `Catalog` sequentially lists the directory of a disk. The listing is made on the printer.

```
1    program Catalog;
2
3      type
4        Str14 = string[14];
5        Str164 = string[164];
6      var
7        Fib : Str164;
8        Dummy : Str14;
9        n, i, position, adr : integer;
10       ok : boolean;
11   (*$U+*)
12
13     procedure Make_Name;
14
15     begin
16       i := i * 32 + adr + 37;
17       position := 1;
18       for n := i + 1 to i + 11 do
19         begin
20           Dummy[position] := chr(mem[n]);
21           position := postion + 1
22         end;
23       Dummy := chr(mem[i] + 65) + ':' +
                    copy(Dummy, 1, 8) + '.' +
                    copy(Dummy, 9, 3);
24       writeln(LST, Dummy);
25     end;
26
27     function CatBegin : boolean;
28
29     begin
30       CatBegin := false;
31       adr := addr(Fib);
32       Dummy := '&:????????.???'
```

```
33          Fib := '??????????';
34          mem[adr] := 164;
35          bdos(26, adr + 37);
36          i := bdos(17, adr + 1);
37          if i <> $FF then
38             begin
39                Make_Name;
40                CatBegin := true
41             end;
42       end;
43
44       function CatNext : boolean;
45
46       begin
47          CatNext := false;
48          adr := addr(Fib);
49          Dummy := '&:????????.???';
50          bdos(26, adr + 37);
51          i := bdos(18, adr + 1);
52          if i <> $FF then
53             begin
54                Make_Name;
55                CatNext := true
56             end;
57       end;
58
59    begin
60       bdos(13);
61       ok := CatBegin;
62       while ok do
63          ok := CatNext;
64       bdos(13)
65    end.
```

In the main program block, BDOS routine 13 is called to reset the disk drive. Next, the boolean function CatBegin is invoked. This function searches for the first entry in the disk directory. First the address of the file interface block (addr(Fib)) is determined.

The DMA address is set to position 37 of the string variable Fib with BDOS function 26.

Using BDOS function 17, the first entry in the directory is found and stored at position 1 of the Fib. If the search is sucessful, i will not be equal to hex FF and the procedure Make_Name is called.

In the procedure Make_Name, the internal representation of a filename is decoded, assigned to the string variable Dummy and printed.

In the **while**-loop of the main program, the function CatNext is called until the last catalog entry has been read. The function CatNext works similarly to the function CatBegin, the difference being that access is made to the variable Fib initialized by CatBegin and the next entry of the directory is stored in it.

Finally, another disk reset is performed. The program also lists the names of deleted files. They are shown with a "&" as the drive name.

7.2 *Dir* procedure for MS-DOS

First we'll explain the functions and procedures SetDTA, CatFirst, and CatNext because these are also used in the procedure tree and are specified as include files.

Procedure SetDTA defines a data buffer for the data transfer during file accesses. It reserves an area of memory at the address passed to it as a paramter (Disk Transfer Address, DTA). The entries of the file table are stored in this data buffer in the following manner:

BYTE	MEANING
00-20	Reseverved for future accesses.
21	The file attribute.
22-23	Time
24-25	Date
26-27	File size, low-order portion
28-29	File size, high-order portion
30-42	Filename

Save to disk under the name **setdta**

```
1     procedure SetDTA(sg,os:integer);
2
3     type regtype = record
4                      ax,bx,cx,dx,bp,
5                      di,si,ds,es,flags : integer;
6                    end;
7
8     var register : regtype;
9         ah       : byte;
10
11    begin
12
13       ah := $1A;
```

```
14
15      with register do
16        begin
17          ax := ah shl 8;
18          ds := sg;
19          dx := os;
20          msdos(register);
21        end;
22    end;
```

The function `CatFirst` searches for the first entry in the directory and returns the value `true` if it finds one. Here we access the ROM BIOS function $4E which requires an unopened FCB. There is another ROM BIOS function, $1E, which has the same function but requires an open FCB.

An FCB (File Control Block) is a storage area used by the operating system. An open FCB contains information about that file: its name, its length, the disk address of the first sector of data, and much more. In order to access the data in a file, the FCB must be opened. But for the purpose of reading the directory, an opened FCB is unnecessary work for the programmer.

An unopened FCB, on the other hand, is simply a string of characters containing the drive specification and path. This is passed to both the function `CatFirst` and `CatNext` as a parameter. The path may be up to 64 bytes long, which is why we declared the variable `str` as `string[64]`.

Save to disk under the name **catfirst**

```
1     function CatFirst(str : str64) : boolean;
2
3     type regtype = record
4                       ax,bx,cx,dx,bp,
5                       di,si,ds,es,flags : integer;
6                    end;
7
8     var register : regtype;
9         ah       : byte;
10
```

```
11    begin
12
13      str := str + '\*.*' + chr(0);
14
15      ah := $4E;
16
17      with register do
18        begin
19          ax := ah shl 8;
20          cx := $10;
21          ds := seg(str);
22          dx := ofs(str)+1;
23          msdos(register);
24          CatFirst:=lo(ax)=0;
25        end;
26    end;
```

Function CatNext searches for the next entry in the directory and returns the value false if no more entries are found.

Save to disk under the name **catnext**

```
1     function CatNext : boolean;
2
3     type regtype = record
4                      ax,bx,cx,dx,bp,
5                      di,si,ds,es,flags : integer;
6                    end;
7
8     var register : regtype;
9         ah       : byte;
10
11    begin
12
13      ah := $4F;
14
```

```
15      with register do
16        begin
17          ax := ah shl 8;
18          cx := $10;
19          msdos(register);
20          CatNext:=lo(ax)=0;
21        end;
22    end;
```

You may have noticed that the cx register is initialized to $10 in both programs (in addition to the ah register which contains the function number). The attribute of the file to be searched for is passed in this register.

DOS 2.0 recognizes seven different file attributes, of which only $20 and $10 are relevant for our purpose. All of the files entered in the directory are given the attribute $20. The attribute $10 indicates a subdirectory. In the procedure Dir, byte 21 of the DTA is checked, and if it is equal to $10, the suffix <DIR> is printed to indicate the subdirectory.

Save to disk under the name **dir.prc**

```
1     procedure Dir (var z);
2
3       type
4         str64 = string[64];
5         str10 = string[10];
6         ar50 = array[0..50] of byte;
7
8       var
9         sg, os : integer;
10        atr : byte;
11        ar : ar50;
12        path : str64;
13        name : str10;
14        ext : str10;
15        time : str10;
16        date : str10;
17        len : str10;
18        cap, fre : real;
19        num : byte;
```

```
20
21    {$I SetDTA}
22    {$I CatFirst}
23    {$I CatNext}
24    {$I DiskPar}                    {see Section 7.6}
25    {$I CurDrive}                   {see Section 7.7}
26
27      procedure htnt (var l : str10);
28
29        var
30          ht, nt : real;
31          n : str10;
32
33      begin
34        l := ' ';
35        nt := ar[27] * 1;
36        nt := nt * 256 + ar[28];
37        str(nt : 0 : 0, n);
38
39        if ht > 0 then
40          begin
41            ht := ar[29] * 1;
42            ht := ht * 256 + ar[30];
43            str(ht : 0 : 0, 1);
44          end;
45
46        l := l + n;
47      end;
48
49      procedure tmdt (var tm, dt : str10);
50
51        var
52          dy, mn, yr : byte;
53          hr, mi, se : byte;
54          sr : str10;
55
56      begin
57        dy := ar[24] and $1f;
58        mn := ((ar[25] shl 8 + ar[24]) and $01e0)
                 shr 5;
59        yr := ar[25] shr 1 + 80;
60
61        hr := ar[23] shr 3;
```

```
62          mi := ((ar[23] shl 8 + ar[22]) and $07ff)
                    shr 5;
63          se := (ar[22] and $1f)*2;
64
65          str(mn, sr);
66          if mn < 10 then
67             sr := ' ' + sr;
68          dt := sr + '-';
69
70          str(dy, sr);
71          if tg < 10 then
72             sr := '0' + sr;
73          dt := dt + sr + '-';
74
75          str(yr, sr);
76          dt := dt + sr;
77
78          str(hr, sr);
79          if hr < 10 then
80             sr := ' ' + sr;
81          tm := sr + ':';
82
83
84          str(mi, sr);
85          if mi < 10 then
86             sr := '0' + sr;
87          tm := tm + sr + ':';
88
89          str(se, sr);
90          if se < 10 then
91             sr := '0' + sr;
92          tm := tm + sr;
93       end;
94
95       procedure Make_Name (var name, ext :
                              str10);
96
97          var
98             i : byte;
99
100      begin
101         i := 30;
102         name := '';
103         ext := '';
```

```
104
105
106        while (ar[i] <> 0) and (chr(ar[i]) <>
                    '.') and (i > 13) do
107          begin
108            name := name + chr(ar[i]);
109            i := i + 1;
110          end;
111
112
113        if ar[i] = ord('.') then
114          begin
115            i := i + 1;
116            while (ar[i] <> 0) and (i < 43) do
117              begin
118                ext := ext + chr(ar[i]);
119                i := i + 1;
120              end;
121          end;
122
123      end;
124
125    begin
126      sg := seg(z);
127      os := ofs(z);
128      move(z,path,mem[sg:os]+1);
129
130      sg := seg(ar);
131      os := ofs(ar);
132      SetDTA(sg, os);
133      num := 0;
134
135      if CatFirst(path) then
136        repeat
137          if (ar[21] <> 16) or (chr(ar[30]) <>
                    '.') then
138            begin
139              tmdt(time, date);
140              htnt(len);
141              Make_Name(name, ext);
142              atr := ar[21];
143
144              gotoxy(1, wherey);
145              write(name);
```

```
146              gotoxy(10, wherey);
147              write(ext);
148              gotoxy(14, wherey);
149
150              if atr = 16 then
151                 write('<dir>')
152              else
153                 write(len : 8);
154
155              gotoxy(24, wherey);
156              write(date);
157              gotoxy(35, wherey);
158              writeln(time);
159              num := num + 1;
160           end;
161        until not CatNext;
162
163     if diskpar(CurDrive, cap, fre) then
164        writeln(num : 10, ' file(s)     ',
                   fre : 0 : 0, ' bytes free');
165
166   end;
```

In the list of formal parameters for the procedure Dir you see a typeless variable. Thanks to this method, the user is not forced to declare a specific type. The parameter must be a string variable (not a constant) containing the drive specifier and path name.

The variable declaration ar of type array[0..50] of byte allows us to access the data buffer in an indexed manner. In lines 126-128 the typeless variable containing the path name is copied into the local variable path.

If function CatFirst returns the value true in line 135, then the first entry is in the buffer and we can read the attribute byte and the starting letter of the filename (137). If the attribute is $10 indicating a subdirectory, but the filename starts with ".", we do not treat it as a subdirectory because it is the reference found in every directory to the directory just above it in the hierarchy. If this is the case, the if block is not executed and nothing is printed.

All of the specifications in the entry are converted to string format. This makes it easier to search for specific entries. We have already seen this in the first statement of the **if** block. The procedure `tmdt` passes the time and date of the file creation or update to the variables of the same names.

The length of the file is divided into two integer numbers where the seventh bit must not be interpreted as a sign bit. For this reason the numbers are first converted to individual characters then combined into one string (line 92). The apparently useless multiplication by 1 here actually performs the type conversion. If you do the following: `ar[27] * 256`, an overflow would occur, meaning that the result would be negative. This is described again in detail in section 7.4.

The filename is created in the procedure `make_name` in which the extension is stored in a special variable. The variable `atr` is assigned the file attribute and the output can begin.

In line 144 a decision is made to see if the suffix <DIR> should be printed to indicate a subdirectory or if the file length should be printed. At the end, the number of files found and the remaining storage space on the diskette are printed. The functions `CurDrive` and `DiskPar`, which permit us to do this are explained in the following sections.

The output is made to the system output when `Dir` is called from the system level.

7.3 *Tree* procedure for MS-DOS

The procedure Tree allows you to display the tree of directories of a diskette or hard disk on the screen. The output is the same as the output of the Tree command which is called from the system level.

Save to disk under the name **tree.prc**

```
1    procedure tree (var z);
2
3      type
4        str64 = string[64];
5        str12 = string[12];
6        ar50 = array[0..50] of byte;
7        ar112 = array[1..112] of str12;
8
9      var
10       sg, os : integer;
11       ar : ar50;
12       path : str64;
13
14   {$i SetDTA.prc}
15   {$i CatFirst.fnc}
16   {$i CatNext.fnc}
17
18     procedure Make_Name (var name : str12);
19
20       var
21         i : byte;
22
23     begin
24       i := 30;
25       name := '';
26       while (ar[i] <> 0) and (i < 43) do
27         begin
28           name := name + chr(ar[i]);
29           i := i + 1;
30         end;
31     end;
32
```

```
33        procedure recur (str : str64);
34          var
35            l, i : byte;
36            sd : ar112;
37
38        begin
39          l := 0;
40          writeln('path:\', str);
41          writeln;
42          writeln('subdirectories :');
43
44          if CatFirst(str) then
45            begin
46              repeat
47                if (ar[21] = 16) and (ar[30] <>
                        ord('.')) then
48                  begin
49                    l := l + 1;
50                    Make_Name(sd[1]);
51                  end;
52              until not CatNext;
53              if l > 0 then
54                begin
55                  for i := 1 to l do
56                    writeln(sd[i]);
57                  writeln;
58                  writeln;
59                  for i := 1 to l do
60                    recur(str + '\' + sd[i], ar);
61                end
62              else
63                begin
64                  writeln('none   ');
65                  writeln;
66                  writeln;
67                end
68            end
69          else
70            begin
71              writeln('none   ');
72              writeln;
73              writeln;
74            end;
75        end;
```

```
76
77   begin
78      sg := seg(z);
79      os := ofs(z);
80      move(z,path,mem[sg:os]+1);
81
82      sg := seg(ar);
83      os := ofs(ar);
84      SetDTA(sg, os);
85
86      recur(path);
87   end;
```

After a DTA is defined in line 80, the procedure `recur` is called. The search and output of the paths is done recursively.

A check is made in lines 47-51 to see if the entry found is a reference to a subdirectory. If this is the case, the filename is created and placed in the variable `sv` of type `array[1..112] of str12`. A dynamic data structure is not needed since a directory can have a maximum of 112 entries.

The subdirectories pertaining to the path are displayed in lines 59-60.

Finally, the procedure `recur` is called in a **for**-loop for each subdirectory found. Here the current path is passed as a parameter which will be extended by the name of a subdirectory.

7.4 *SetDrive* procedure

The current drive can be set with this procedure. This is done by passing the drive number to the procedure SetDrive. Drive A has the number 0, drive B the number 1, and so on.

Save to disk under the name **setdrive.prc**

```
1    procedure SetDrive (dn : byte);
2
3    type regtype = record
4                     ax,bx,cx,dx,bp,
5                     di,si,ds,es,flags : integer;
6                   end;
7
8    var register : regtype;
9        ah        : byte;
10
11   begin
12      ah := $0E;
13
14      with register do
15        begin
16          ax := ah shl 8;
17          dx := dn;
18          msdos(register);
19        end;
20   end;
```

The procedure uses the MS-DOS function $0E to set the current drive. Before calling the MS-DOS procedure, the high-order byte of the ax register is loaded with the function number and the low-order byte of the dx register is loaded with the drive number.

7.5 *ChDir* function

Function ChDir changes the current file directory. A string variable containing the drive specification and path is passed to the routine as an argument. ChDir returns the value true if the specified directory is valid.

Save to disk under the name **chdir.fnc**

```
1     function ChDir(var z) : boolean;
2
3     type regtype = record
4                      ax,bx,cx,dx,bp,
5                      di,si,ds,es,flags : integer;
6                    end;
7
8     var register : regtype;
9         ah        : byte;
10        str       : string[64];
11
12    begin
13      move(z,str,mem[seg(z):ofs(z)]+1;
14      str := str+chr(0);
15
16      ah := $3B;
17
18      with register do
19        begin
20          ax := ah shl 8;
21          ds := seg(str);
22          dx := ofs(str)+1;
23          msdos(register);
24          ChDir:=lo(ax)=0;
25        end;
26    end;
```

In lines 13 and 14 and the contents of the current parameter are copied to the string variable str. The string must be terminated with chr(0). In line 20 the high-order byte of the ax register is loaded with the number of the MS-DOS function $3B. Before calling the MS-DOS procedure, the ds register is loaded with the segment address and the low-order byte of the dx register is loaded with offset plus one of str, because the first byte of str contains the length of the string variable and is not an element of the string.

7.6 *DiskPar* function

We can use this function to determine the capacity as well as the remaining space on the diskette or hard disk.

Save to disk under the name **diskpar.fnc**

```
1     function DiskPar (dl:byte;var cp,fr:real)
                        :boolean;
2
3     type regtype = record
4                       ax,bx,cx,dx,bp,
5                       di,si,ds,es,flags : integer;
6                    end;
7
8     var register : regtype;
9         ah       : byte;
10
11    begin
12      ah := $36;
13      with register do
14        begin
15          ax := ah shl 8;
16          dx := dl;
17          msdos(register);
18          DiskPar := ax<>$FFFF;
19          cp      := ax*cx;
20          fr      := cp*bx;
21          cp      := cp*dx;
22        end;
23    end;
```

Function `DiskPar` uses the DOS function $36. The function number is loaded into the `ax` register and the drive number into the `dx` register. After calling the MS-DOS procedure, the number of bytes per sector is found in the `cx` register, the number of sectors per cluster in the `ax` register, the number of clusters in the `dx` registers, and the number of free clusters in the `bx` register. If we multiply the contents of `ax` and `cx` we get the number of bytes per cluster.

We assign the result to a real variable and multiply it by the contents of the bx register in order to obtain the number of free bytes. The capacity of the diskette or hard disk is determined by multiplying the result by the contents of the dx register. The number of bytes per cluster can be represented as an integer number. Before we calculate the number of free bytes or the capacity, however, we convert this to real to avoid possible overflow from distorting the result.

If a valid drive number is passed as a parameter, ax contains the number of sectors per cluster. Otherwise the number $FFFF is found in ax and the values returned are invalid.

7.7 *CurDrive* function

Function CurDrive returns the actual drive number from which the drive specification can be derived.

Save to disk under the name **curdrive.fnc**

```
1    function CurDrive : byte;
2
3    type regtype = record
4                     ax,bx,cx,dx,bp,
5                     di,si,ds,es,flags : integer;
6                   end;
7
8    var register : regtype;
9        ah       : byte;
10
11   begin
12     ah := $19;
13     with register do
14       begin
15         ax := ah shl 8;
16         msdos(register);
17         CurDrive:=lo(ax);
18       end;
19   end;
```

The function uses DOS function $19. In line 12 the function number is loaded into ah and assigned to the ax register in line 15. After calling the MS-DOS procedure, the low-order byte of the ax register contains the drive number which is then assigned to the function variable in line 17. If you want to get the drive specification as the result, define CurDrive as a function of type char and replace line 17 with:

```
CurDrive:=chr(ord('A')+lo(ax));
```

CHAPTER 8

Chapter 8: Time and Date - using MS-DOS

8.1 *SetTime* procedure

This procedure allows the programmer to set the system clock. It is called with four parameters:

1. Hours   0 to 23
2. Minutes   0 to 59
3. Seconds   0 to 59
4. Hundreths 0 to 99

```
1    procedure SetTime(hour,min,sec,hsec:byte);
2
3    type regtype = record
4                       ax,bx,cx,dx,bp,
5                       di,si,ds,es,flags : integer;
6                   end;
7
8    var register : regtype;
9        ah       : byte;
10
11   begin
12     ah := $2D;
13
14   with register do
15     begin
16       ax := ah shl 8;
17       cx := hour shl 8 + min;
18       dx := sec  shl 8 + hsec;
19       msdos(register);
20     end;
21   end;
```

The procedure uses the MS-DOS function $2D for setting the system time. Before calling the MS-DOS procedure the function number is loaded into the high-order byte of the ax register.

167

The high-order byte of the `cx` register contains the hours and the low-order byte the minutes. The seconds are stored in the high-order byte of the `dx` register and the hundreths in the low-order byte.

These registers are loaded with the appropriate data in lines 16 and 18.

8.2 *GetTime* procedure

This procedure lets the programmer access the system time. All parameters must be of type `byte` and passed by reference.

```
1    procedure GetTime(var hour,min,sec,hsec
                          :byte);
2
3    type regtype = record
4                     ax,bx,cx,dx,bp,
5                     di,si,ds,es,flags : integer;
6                   end;
7
8    var register : regtype;
9        ah       : byte;
10
11   begin
12     ah := $2C;
13
14     with register do
15       begin
16         ax := ah shl 8;
17         MsDos(register);
18         hour := hi(cx);
19         min  := lo(cx);
20         sec  := hi(dx);
21         hsec := lo(dx);
22       end;
23   end;
```

The procedure uses the MS-DOS function $2C to access the system time. The contents of the CPU registers, are returned in the parameters and have the same meaning as that described earlier for the SetTime procedure.

8.3 *SetDate* procedure

The procedure SetDate isused to set the system date. The procedure is called with three parameters:

1. Day   1 to 31
2. Month   1 to 12
3. Year   1980 to 2099

```
1    procedure SetDate(day,month:byte;year:
                       integer);
2
3    type regtype = record
4                        ax,bx,cx,dx,bp,
5                        di,si,ds,es,flags : integer;
6                   end;
7
8    var register : regtype;
9        ah        : byte;
10
11   begin
12     ah := $2B;
13
14   with register do
15     begin
16       ax := ah shl 8;
17       cx := year;
18       dx := month shl 8 + day;
19       msdos(register);
20     end;
21   end;
```

The procedure `SetDate` uses the MS-DOS function number $2B for setting the system date.

The year is placed in the `cx` register as a binary value. The month is placed in the high-order byte of the `dx` register and the day in the low-order byte.

The registers are assigned the values of the parameters in lines 16 to 18.

8.4 *GetDate* procedure

This procedure accesses the system date. It's called with three parameters. The first two are of type `byte` and the third of type `integer`.

```
1    procedure GetDate(var day,month:byte;var
                              year:integer);
2
3    type regtype = record
4                          ax,bx,cx,dx,bp,
5                          di,si,ds,es,flags : integer;
6                       end;
7
8    var register : regtype;
9        ah        : byte;
10
11   begin
12     ah := $2A;
13
14     with register do
15       begin
16         ax := ah shl 8;
17         MsDos(register);
18         day   := lo(dx);
19         month := hi(dx);
20         year  := cx;
21       end;
22   end;
```

To access the date, MS-DOS function number $2A is used. Before the procedure is called, this number is loaded into the high-order byte of the `ax` register.

The contents of the CPU registers are then assigned to the appropriate parameters (lines 18 to 20).

CHAPTER 9

Chapter 9: Utilities to use with Turbo

This chapter presents three utilities that can make programming with Turbo Pascal easier and more productive.

The utilites are:

1. *ProgramLister* for listing Turbo programs in an orderly way.
2. *Xref* for cross-referencing variables and keywords usage.
3. *Tracer* for helping you to debug your Turbo programs.

9.1 *ProgramLister* - a utility for listing programs

This program, `ProgramLister` makes it easy to list your Turbo Pascal source files. In contrast to `TLIST`, the program included on the Turbo Pascal diskette, our `ProgramLister` can be adapted to work with any printer. This adaptation, which we'll describe in detail, requires only appropriate changes to the constant declaration portion of the program.

`ProgramLister` also allows a large number of user-selectable options which make it more flexible than `TLIST`.

After starting `ProgramLister`, you will be asked for the following information:

1. Filename
   Enter the complete name of the file to be printed including the extension. The program searches for the file on the disk as soon as you press the RETURN key. If the file is not present, you must reenter the filename.

2. Line numbering (y/n)
   You can select whether or not the program lines should be numbered or not. The program lister also numbers blank lines.

3. Page numbering (y/n)
   By selecting y, all of the pages are numbered starting with page 1. The page number, in the form `Page x`, appears in the upper right-hand corner of the page.

4. Print title (y/n)
    You can choose whether or not to print a title. If you answer y, a title consisting of the filename and the name of the program, procedure, or function is printed at the top of each page in parentheses.

5. Emphasize keywords (y/n)
    When printing the source text you have the option of emphasizing the keywords like **Begin, Procedure,** etc. This increases the readability of the program listing.

6. Print include files (y/n)
    B answering y, all include files are printed in their entirety in the listing.

7. Nesting depth (y/n)
    The nesting depth of a procedure or function can be printed answer y. In addition, the name of the block preceding it is printed.

    After selecting from among these options, the printing begins. It can be interrupted at any time by pressing Ctrl-C.

    As we've already mentioned, the program lister can be adapted for any printer. This is done by assigning the appropriate printer control characters to the constants. The following constants can be changed:

Constant	Purpose
slg	Number of lines to be printed per page.
empon	Printer control character for emphasizing the keywords.
empoff	Control character which turns the emphasis off.
lnon	Control character which determines the appearance of the line numbers.
lnoff	This control character switches back to normal print.
pnon	With this control character the print style for the "Page x" can be changed.
pnoff	Switches back to normal print.

tion	Sets the print style with which the title is printed.
tioff	Switches back to normal print.
pron	Sets the print style in which the nesting depth is printed.
proff	Switches back to normal print.
normon	Sets the print style in which the usual text will be printed.
normoff	Switched the style selected by `normon` off again.
tabl	Sets the left margin.
lnlg	Sets the number of digits of which line numbers consist.
pnlg	Sets the number of digits for the page number.
charset	Control characters which select the printer's character set.
svor	Control character for the form feed.

The following procedures are used in all of the utility programs, so we list them separately here. They are included as `include` files in the various programs.

Functions and Procedure used by *ProgramLister*:

Save to disk under the name **status.fnc**

```
1     function status (ws : field;
2                        ss : byte) : boolean;
3     begin
4       if not mode then
5          begin
6            if (ws[ss] = '''') and (paren = 0)
                 then
7              mode := not mode
8            else
9              begin
10               if (ws[ss] = '{') or (ws[ss] =
                     '(*') then
11                 begin
12                   ss := ss + 1;
13                   if (((ws[ss] = '$I') or
                       (ws[ss] = '$i'))) and
                         iflag then
14                     begin
15                       ss := ss + 1;
16                       if not (ws[ss][1] in
                           ['+', '-']) then
17                         begin
18                           InFile := ws[ss + 1];
19                           includ := true;
20                         end
21                       else
22                         paren := paren + 1;
23                     end
24                   else
25                     paren := paren + 1;
26               end
```

```
27              else if ((ws[ss] = '}') or (ws[ss]
                        = '*)')) and not includ then
28                paren := paren - 1;
29            end
30        end
31      else if ws[ss] = '''' then
32        mode := not mode;
33
34      status := not (mode or includ or
                      (paren > 0));
35    end;
```

Save to disk under the name **search.fnc**

```
1     function search (var b) : boolean;
2       type
3         ky = array[1..37] of string[15];
4
5     const keys:ky=('and','array','begin','case',
6           'const','div','downto','else',
7           'end','file','for','forward',
8           'function','goto','if','in',
9           'label','mod','procedure','do',
10          'nil','not','of','or','packed',
11          'program','record','repeat',
12          'set','then','to','type',
13          'until','var','while','with',
14          'external');
15
16      var
17        i : integer;
18        bf : string[80];
19
20    begin
21    move(b,bf,mem[seg(b):ofs(b)]+1);
22    { move(b,bf,mem[addr(b)]+1); CP/M only}
23      i := 0;
24      repeat
25        i := succ(i);
26      until (i >= 37) or (bf = keys[i]);
27
28      search := (bf = keys[i]);
29    end;
```

Save to disk under the name **field_in.prc**

```
1     procedure field_in (var z;
2                         var ww : field;
3                         var max : byte);
4
5        const special:trz=['{','}','(',')','*',
6                           ''''];
7              alfa:trz=['a'..'z','A'..'Z','^','$'];
8              digalf:trz=['a'..'z','A'..'Z',
                           '0'..'9','^','$','_'];
9
10       var
11         pw : byte;
12         zw : string[80];
13
14    begin
15       move(z,zw,mem[seg(z):ofs(z)]+1);
16       { move(z,zw,mem[addr(z)]+1); CP/M only}
17       pw := 1;
18       max := 0;
19       while pw <= length(zw) do
20         begin
21           max := succ(max);
22           ww[max] := '';
23           if not (zw[pw] in alfa) then
24             begin
25               if not (zw[pw] in special) then
26                 begin
27                   repeat
28                     ww[max] := ww[max] + zw[pw];
29                     pw := succ(pw);
30                   until (zw[pw] in (alfa +
                         special)) or (pw > length(zw))
31                 end
32               else
33                 begin
34                   ww[max] := ww[max] + zw[pw];
35                   pw := succ(pw);
```

```
36                  if ((ww[max] = '(') and
                        (zw[pw] = '*')) or
                       ((ww[max] = '*') and
                        (zw[pw] = ')')) then
37                    begin
38                      ww[max] := ww[max] +
                                    zw[pw];
39                      pw := succ(pw);
40                    end;
41                end;
42            end
43          else
44            begin
45              repeat
46                ww[max] := ww[max] + zw[pw];
47                pw := succ(pw);
48              until (pw > length(zw)) or
                    not ((zw[pw] in digalf) or
                         ((zw[pw] = '.') and
                          (zw[pw + 1] in digalf)))
49            end;
50        end;
51    end;
```

179

Listing of *ProgramLister* :

Save to disk under the name *lister.pas*

```
1     program ProgramLister;
2
3       const
4         slg = 64;
5         llg = 79;
6         empon = ^['E';
7         empoff = ^['F';
8         lnon = '';
9         lnoff = '';
10        pnon = ^['E';
11        pnoff = ^['F';
12        tion = ^['4';
13        tioff = ^['5';
14        pron = ^['4'^['E';
15        proff = ^['5'^['F';
16        normon = '';
17        normoff = '';
18        tabl = 0;
19        lnlg = 4;
20        pnlg = 2;
21        charset = ^['R'^@;
22        svor = ^L;
23
24      type
25        str80 = string[80];
26        str15 = string[15];
27        str12 = string[12];
28        field = array[1..80] of str80;{60 CP/M}
29        trz = set of char;
30
31      var
32        includ, mode : boolean;
33        kflag, hflag, prc : boolean;
34        iflag, vflag : boolean;
35        pflag, zflag : boolean;
36        line, title : str80;
37        InFile : str12;
38        pnum, lnum : str15;
39        pnumber, lnumber, lnr : integer;
40        pronam : array[0..10] of str80;
```

```
41          blk : array[1..100] of str12; {75 CP/M}
42          source, inclsource : text;
43          paren : byte;
44          proc, beg, indmax : byte;
45          target : text;
46          word : field;
47          edge, tbstr, lnstr : str15;
48          ch : char;
49
50     {$I open_r.fnc}
51
52     {$I search.fnc}
53
54       procedure pretitle (var k : str80;
55                           fl : boolean);
56       var
57          space, zs : str80;
58          sp : byte;
59
60     begin
61        sp := 1;
62        zs := '';
63
64        if fl then
65          begin
66            while not (k[sp] in [';', '(']) do
67              begin
68                zs := zs + k[sp];
69                sp := succ(sp);
70              end;
71            zs := zs + ' ' + '(' + InFile + ')';
72          end;
73
74        sp := llg - length(zs);
75        if pflag then
76          sp := sp - 5 - pnlg;
77
78        fillchar(k, sp, ' ');
79        sp := sp - 1;
80        move(sp, k, 1);
81        insert(zs, k, sp div 2);
82        k := tbstr + k;
83     end;
84
```

```
85     {$I field_in.prc}
86
87       procedure field_out (wl : field;
88                            max : byte);
89         var
90           buffer : str80;
91           sl : byte;
92
93     {$I status.fnc}
94
95         procedure vprint (wv : field;
96                           sl : byte);
97
98         begin
99           if (wv[sl] = 'procedure') or
                 (wv[sl] = 'function') then
100             begin
101               if proc > 0 then
102                 begin
103                   write(lst, lnstr, 'ND = ',
                          proc - 1, '    ');
104                   if proc > 1 then
105                     writeln(lst, pron,
                            pronam[proc - 1], proff)
106                   else
107                     writeln(lst);
108                   write(lst, tbstr);
109                   lnr := lnr + 1;
110                 end;
111             end;
112         end;
113
114         procedure vlevel (wv : field;
115                           sl : byte);
116
117         begin
118           if (wv[sl] = 'procedure') or
                 (wv[sl] = 'function') or
                 (wv[sl] = 'program') then
119             begin
120               pronam[proc] := wv[sl] + wv[sl + 1]
                                  + wv[sl + 2];
121               proc := succ(proc);
122             end
```

```
123            else if (wv[sl] = 'begin') or
                       (wv[sl] = 'case') or
                       (wv[sl] = 'record') then
124            begin
125              beg := succ(beg);
126              blk[beg] := wv[sl];
127            end
128            else if (wv[sl] = 'end') then
129            begin
130              beg := pred(beg);
131              if (beg = 0) and
                     (blk[1] = 'begin') then
132                proc := pred(proc);
133            end
134            else if wv[sl] = 'external' then
135              proc := pred(proc);
136          end;
137
138
139     begin
140        sl := 1;
141        if max > 0 then
142          begin
143            if vflag and search(wl[sl]) then
144              if status(wl, sl) then
145                vprint(wl, sl);
146          end;
147
148        if zflag then
149          begin
150            str(lnumber, lnum);
151            write(lst, lnon, lnum, lnoff);
152            edge := copy(lnstr, 1, lnlg -
                              length(lnum));
153            write(lst, edge);
154          end;
155
156        while sl <= max do
157          begin
158            if (status(wl, sl)) and
                   search(wl[sl]) then
```

```
159                  begin
160                    if hflag then
161                       write(lst, empon, wl[sl],
                                    empoff)
162                    else
163                       write(lst, normon, wl[sl],
                                    normoff);
164                     vlevel(wl, sl);
165                    end
166                  else if not includ then
167                     write(lst, normon, wl[sl],
                                 normoff);
168                  sl := sl + 1;
169             end;
170        end;
171
172        procedure init;
173
174        begin
175          repeat
176            repeat
177              clrscr;
178              writeln;
179
180              buflen := 15;
181              write('Filename                : ');
182              readln(InFile);
183              writeln;
184            until open_r(source, InFile);
185
186            buflen := 1;
187            write('Line numbering      (y/n) : ');
188            readln(ch);
189            ch := upcase(ch);
190            zflag := ch = 'Y';
191            writeln;
192
193            buflen := 1;
194            write('Page numbering      (y/n) : ');
195            readln(ch);
196            ch := upcase(ch);
197            pflag := ch = 'Y';
198            writeln;
199
```

```
200             buflen := 1;
201             write('Print title          (y/n) : ');
202             readln(ch);
203             ch := upcase(ch);
204             kflag := ch = 'Y';
205             writeln;
206
207             buflen := 1;
208             write('Emphasize keywords   (y/n) : ');
209             readln(ch);
210             ch := upcase(ch);
211             hflag := ch = 'Y';
212             writeln;
213
214             buflen := 1;
215             write('Print include files  (y/n) : ');
216             readln(ch);
217             ch := upcase(ch);
218             iflag := ch = 'Y';
219             writeln;
220
221             buflen := 1;
222             write('Show nesting         (y/n) : ');
223             readln(ch);
224             ch := upcase(ch);
225             vflag := ch = 'Y';
226             writeln;
227
228             buflen := 1;
229             write('Input correct        (y/n) : ');
230             readln(ch);
231             ch := upcase(ch);
232
233         until ch = 'Y';
234
235
236         paren := 0;
237         mode := false;
238         includ := false;
239
240         lnr := 0;
241         lnumber := 0;
242         pnumber := 1;
243         proc := 0;
```

```
244        beg := 0;
245
246        pnum := '';
247        lnum := '';
248        title := '';
249
250        fillchar(tbstr, tabl + 1, ' ');
251        tbstr[0] := chr(tabl);
252        fillchar(lnstr, lnlg + 1, ' ');
253        lnstr[0] := chr(lnlg);
254
255        if not eof(source) then
256          begin
257            readln(source, title);
258            pretitle(title, kflag);
259            reset(source);
260          end;
261
262        write(lst, charset);
263      end;
264
265
266      procedure printout (var insource : text);
267      begin
268        InFile := '';
269        while not eof(insource) do
270          begin
271            if ((lnr + slg) mod slg) = 0 then
272              begin
273                if kflag or pflag then
274                  begin
275                    write(lst, tion, title,
276                          tioff);
276                    if pflag then
277                      begin
278                        str(pnumber, pnum);
279                        pnum := 'page ' + pnum;
280                        write(lst, pnon, pnum,
281                              pnoff);
281                        pnumber := pnumber + 1;
282                      end;
283                    writeln(lst);
284                    writeln(lst);
285                    lnr := lnr + 2;
```

```
286                      end;
287                   end;
288
289             lnumber := succ(lnumber);
290
291             line := '';
292             readln(insource, line);
293             field_in(line, word, indmax);
294             write(lst, tbstr);
295
296
297             field_out(word, indmax);
298             writeln(lst);
299             lnr := lnr + 1;
300             if includ then
301               begin
302                 includ := false;
303                 if open_r(inclsource,InFile)
                        then
304                   printout(inclsource)
305               end;
306             if ((lnr + slg) mod slg) = 0 then
307                 write(lst, svor);
308           end;
309
310       close(insource);
311     end;
312
313   { main program }
314
315   begin
316     repeat
317       init;
318       printout(source);
319       write(lst, svor);
320       write('Print another program  (y/n)    ');
321       buflen := 1;
322       read(ch);
323     until UpCase(ch) <> 'Y';
324   end.
```

9.2 *Xref* - Cross-reference lister

This utility program creates a cross reference list for Turbo Pascal programs. This list consists of all of the objects declared in the program: constants, variables, procedures, functions, and so on. These objects are printed along with the numbers of the lines in which they are found.

Keywords like **Begin**, **Procedure** and **Function** are also part of the cross-reference list and are printed in bold print.

The cross reference list can be used to help in program documentation or in looking for errors.

After starting the program, you will be asked for the following:

1. Filename
   Enter the name of the Pascal source file for which the cross-reference should be created. As with `ProgramLister`, the complete name including the extension must be entered.

2. Process include files? (y/n)
   You can decide also cross-reference any `include` files that may be part of the program by answering `y`.

3. Output to printer (p)
          diskette (d)
   The cross-reference listing can be sent either to the printer or to a disk file. If the disk output is selected, the program generates a cross-reference list with a filename of the source text file and the extension `.CRF`.

As with *ProgramLister*, you can adapt the *Xref* cross-reference program for any printer. The following constants can be changed to do this:

Constant	Purpose
llg	Line length
slg	Number of lines per page.
numform	Number of digits in a line number.

empon	Control characters to emphasize the keywords.
empoff	Control characters to turn the emphasis off.
lnon	Control characters which determine the print style for the line numbers.
lnoff	Control characters to turn off the print style enabled by `lnon`.
charset	Control characters to select the character set on the printer.
svor	Control character for the form feed.

The following pages contain a sample printout from the *CrossReference* program. It shows a cross-reference listing of the variables and keywords used in the program *CrossReference* (itself).

Sample printout of CrossReference program listing using *Xref*.

```
IOresult          62
InFile            38   383   434   442   457   474   486
^li               19
^wd               18
a                 50    60    61    64   359   408
alfa             107   123   130
and              136   148   242   262   349   371   378   392   409
                 410
array             17    75
assign            60   170
b                 73    93
begin             56    63    92   114   120   124   126   133   137
                 144   160   187   190   197   199   204   213   216
                 225   227   239   243   246   248   263   281   289
                 296   306   308   320   323   328   368   370   374
                 376   379   382   402   405   407   412   430   439
                 473   476   484   498
bf                90    93    98   100
boolean           36    37    51    73   367   427
buffer           362
buflen           432   445   453
byte              43    45   104   111   157   279   357   363   367
                 471
case             310   321   340
char              16    47
charset           10
chr              293
close             64   493   503
clrscr           431
const              2    32    77   106   359
cr                33
crossreference     1
d                 54    57    60   158   161   163   164   168   169
                 170   171
delete           168
digalf           108   148
div              285
do               119   198   242   288   305   404   475
dt                51    57   154   161
else              67   132   143   196   224   235   238   256   259
                 299   302   319   373   386   389   392   396   504
```

190

Xref - listing

```
1    program CrossReference;
2      const
3        llg = 60;
4        slg = 40;
5        numform = 5;
6        empon = ^['E';
7        empoff = ^['F';
8        lnon = '';
9        lnoff = '';
10       charset = ^['R'^@;
11       svor = ^L;
12
13     type
14       str = string[80];
15       wrd = string[20];
16       trz = set of char;
17       field = array[1..80] of wrd;
18       wptr = ^wd;
19       lptr = ^li;
20
21       wd = record
22           nw : wrd;
23           nextw : wptr;
24           nextl : lptr;
25         end;
26       li = record
27           lnn : integer;
28           nextl : lptr;
29         end;
30
31
32     const
33       cr = 'c';
34       ncr = ' ';
35     var
36       includ, iflag : boolean;
37       mode : boolean;
38       InFile : str;
39       source, inclsource : text;
40       target : text;
41       start : wptr;
```

```
42          lnumber : integer;
43          paren : byte;
44          word : field;
45          format : byte;
46          fill : str;
47          out : char;
48
49    {$I open_r.fnc}
50
51    {$I search.fnc}
52
53    {$I field_in.prc}
54
55      procedure open_w (var q : text;
56                        var dt);
57
58        var
59          ln, ps : byte;
60          d : string[12];
61
62      begin
63        move(dt,d,mem[seg(dt):ofs(dt)]+1);
64          { move(dt,d,mem[addr(dt)]+1); CP/M only}
65        ln := length(d);
66        ps := pos('.', d);
67        if (ps = 0) or (ps > 8) then
68          ps := 9;
69
70        delete(d, ps, ln - ps + 1);
71        d := d + '.crf';
72        assign(q, d);
73        writeln(d);
74        rewrite(q);
75
76      end;
77
78      procedure word_in_list (word : wrd;
79                        lnum : integer);
80        var
81          ph, pv : wptr;
82          pw : wptr;
83
```

```
84          procedure lnum_in_list (var z : lptr;
85                           lnn : integer);
86            var
87              zv, zh : lptr;
88
89          begin
90            zv := z;
91            if zv = nil then
92              begin
93                new(zv);
94                zv^.nextl := nil;
95                zv^.lnn := lnn;
96                z := zv;
97              end
98            else
99              begin
100               while zv <> nil do
101                 begin
102                   zh := zv;
103                   zv := zh^.nextl;
104                 end;
105               if zh^.lnn <> lnn then
106                 begin
107                   new(zv);
108                   zv^.nextl := nil;
109                   zv^.lnn := lnn;
110                   zh^.nextl := zv;
111                 end;
112             end;
113         end;
114
115       begin
116         pw := start;
117         if pw = nil then
118           begin
119             new(pw);
120             pw^.nextl := nil;
121             pw^.nw := word;
122             pw^.nextw := start;
123             start := pw;
124             lnum_in_list(pw^.nextl, lnum);
125           end
126         else if word <= pw^.nw then
```

```
127          begin
128            if word < pw^.nw then
129              begin
130                new(pw);
131                pw^.nextl := nil;
132                pw^.nw := word;
133                pw^.nextw := start;
134                start := pw;
135                lnum_in_list(pw^.nextl, lnum);
136              end
137            else
138              lnum_in_list(pw^.nextl, lnum);
139          end
140        else
141          begin
142            pv := start;
143            ph := start;
144            while (pv^.nextw <> nil) and
                    (pv = ph) do
145              begin
146                pv := pv^.nextw;
147                if word <= pv^.nw then
148                  begin
149                    if word < pv^.nw then
150                      begin
151                        new(pw);
152                        pw^.nextl := nil;
153                        pw^.nw := word;
154                        pw^.nextw := pv;
155                        ph^.nextw := pw;
156                        lnum_in_list(pw^.nextl,
                                       lnum);
157                      end
158                    else
159                      lnum_in_list(pv^.nextl,
                                     lnum);
160                  end
161                else
162                  ph := pv;
163              end;
164            if (pv^.nextw = nil) and
                  (word > pv^.nw) then
```

```
165              begin
166                new(pw);
167                pw^.nextl := nil;
168                pw^.nw := word;
169                pw^.nextw := nil;
170                pv^.nextw := pw;
171                lnum_in_list(pw^.nextl, lnum);
172              end;
173            end;
174      end;
175
176
177      procedure outp (top : wptr);
178        var
179          pt : lptr;
180          outstr : str;
181          lf, sf, maxnum : byte;
182
183      begin
184        fillchar(fill, format + 1, ' ');
185        move(format, fill, 1);
186
187        maxnum := (llg - format) div numform;
188
189        sf := 1;
190        while top <> nil do
191          begin
192            lf := 1;
193            outstr := fill;
194            outstr := top^.nw;
195            outstr[0] := chr(format);
196
197            if out = 'P' then
198              begin
199                if search(top^.nw) then
200                  write(lst, empon, outstr,
                            empoff)
201                else
202                  write(lst, outstr);
203              end
204            else
205              write(target, outstr);
206            pt := top^.nextl
```

```
207            while zp <> nil do
208              begin
209                if lf <= maxnum then
210                  begin
211                    str(pt^.lnn : numform,
                           outstr);
212                    case out of
213                      'P' :
214                        write(lst, lnon, outstr,
                                 lnoff);
215                      'D' :
216                        write(target, outstr);
217
218                    pt := pt^.nextl;
219                    lf := succ(lf);
220                  end
221                else
222                  begin
223                    case out of
224                      'P' :
225                        begin
226                          writeln(lst);
227                          write(lst, fill);
228                        end;
229                      'D' :
230                        begin
231                          writeln(target);
232                          write(target, fill);
233                        end;
234                    end;
235
236                    lf := 1;
237                    sf := sf + 1;
238                  end;
239              end;
240            top := top^.nextw;
241
242            case out of
243              'P' :
244                writeln(lst);
245              'D' :
246                writeln(target);
247            end;
248
```

```
249                   sf := sf + 1;
250
251                if ((slg + sf) mod slg = 0) and
                        (out = 'P') then
252                   write(lst, svor);
253             end;
254       end;
255
256
257
258    procedure field_out (wl : field;
259                         max : byte);
260
261    const a : trz = ['a'..'z','A'..'Z'];
262
263       var
264         buffer : str;
265         sl : byte;
266
267  {$I status.fnc}
268
269    begin
270       sl := 1;
271       while sl <= max do
272          begin
273             if status(wl, sl) then
274                begin
275                   if (wl[sl][1] in a) or
276                      ((wl[sl][1] = '^') and
                         (length(wl[sl]) > 1) and
                         (upcase(wl[sl][2]) <>
                         wl[sl][2])) then
276                      begin
277                      word_in_list(wl[sl],
                                      lnumber);
278                         if format<length(wl[sl])
                               then
279                            format := length(wl[sl]);
280                         end
281                   end;
282             sl := sl + 1;
283          end;
284       end;
285
```

```
286
287
288       procedure init;
289
290         var
291           ok : boolean;
292
293         procedure inp;
294         begin
295           clrscr;
296           buflen := 15;
297           write('Filename    : ');
298           readln(InFile);
299         end;
300
301
302
303       begin
304         repeat
305           inp;
306         until open_r(source, InFile);
307
308         write('Process include files  (y/n) : ');
309         buflen := 1;
310         readln(out);
311         writeln;
312         out := upcase(out);
313         iflag := out = 'Y';
314
315         writeln('Output to printer (p)');
316         write('              disk   (d) :');
317         buflen := 1;
318         readln(out);
319         out := upcase(out);
320         if out = 'D' then
321           open_w(target, InFile);
322
323         start := nil;
324         mode := false;
325         includ := false;
326         paren := 0;
327         lnumber := 1;
328         format := 0;
329       end;
```

```
330
331
332        procedure readin (var src : text);
333          var
334            line : str;
335            lf, maxind : byte;
336
337        begin
338          InFile := '';
339          while not eof(src) do
340            begin
341              line := '';
342              readln(src, line);
343              field_in(line, word, maxind);
344              field_out(word, maxind);
345              lnumber := succ(lnumber);
346
347              if includ then
348                begin
349                  includ := false;
350                  if open_r(inclsource, InFile)
                        then
351                    readin(inclsource)
352                end;
353
354
355
356            end;
357          close(src);
358        end;
359
360    {main program}
361
362    begin
363      init;
364      readin(source);
365      outp(start);
366      if out = 'D' then
367        close(target)
368      else
369        write(lst, svor);
370    end.
```

9.3 *Tracer* - a debugging aid

The utility program described here is designed to help you test and debug your Turbo Pascal programs. It can greatly reduce the amount of time you spend testing a program.

Working with the `tracer` consists of first converting the test program into the appropriate form and the actual trace itself.

The program `convert` creates a special source file from your program by inserting special test instructions and control information.

The converted source file to be traced must first be compiled (with the C compiler directive for larger programs) and can then be run. Note that the procedure `menu` is processed as an include file and must be present on the disk under the name `menu.prc`.

The following information is asked for when running `convert`:

1. Filename
   Enter the name of your source file. The extension `.pas` must be part of the filename.

2. Single step mode (y/n)
   The debugger will start with the single-step processing if you answer y. This mode can be changed later during the run.

The program line being processed by `convert` is displayed during the conversion.

When `convert` finished, a file with the name of your program plus the extension `.TRC` is written to the disk.

Compile the this converted program (*filename*.trc). Use the `Com-file` option of `Option` to create an executable program.

After this converted program is compiled, you can run it like any other Turbo program. However, the `Trace` menu will direct you to enter any options.

204

The following information is displayed during the trace:

a) The name of the procedure or function currently being executed

b) The number of the line currently being executed

The trace options can be controlled by the user. Pressing any key causes the trace to stop and you are asked for a command.

The following options are available:

T: Switches between the normal and single-step modes.

L: Prints a listing of all of the procedures and functions and the number of passes made through them. The procedures and functions are printed individually. The space bar can be used to page through the listing.

D: Prints a listing of the procedures and functions declared in the program and the number passses made through them. The list is sent to the printer.

^C: Causes the trace to stop.

By tracing the program CrossReference, and entering the command D, the following list is printed:

```
Program :  CrossReference

Procedure/function          Number of passes
_____

procedure word_in_list          23

procedure lnum_in_list          23

procedure open_w                 0

function open_r                  1
```

```
function search              0

procedure field_in          15

procedure output             0

procedure field_out         15

function status             83

procedure init               1

procedure inp                1

procedure ReadIn             1
```

This list contains valuable information which can be used to optimize the program. For example, `function status` is used 83 times during the course of this run. In order to optimize the program, you would probably want to concentrate on this function.

Convert program - prepares source program for trace

```
 1 program convert;
 2
 3 type str80    = string[100];
 4      str12    = string[12];
 5      arstr80 = array[1..80] of str80;{50]CP/M}
 6      arstr12 = array[0..10] of str12;
 7      trz      = set of char;
 8
 9
10   const a1 = ' menu (1,''';
11         z1 = ''');';
12         a2 = ' menu (2,''';
13         z2 = ''') ';
14         a3 = ' menu (3,''';
15         z3 = ''') ';
16
17         pr1 = 'type aaaa80 = string[40];';
18
19         pr2 = 'var pronam : array[1..50] of
                          aaaa80;'; {[1..30] CP/M}
20         pr3 = '     promem : array[1..50] of
                          aaaa80;'; {[1..30] CP/M}
21         pr4 = '     prozlr : array[1..50] of
                          real;'; {[1..30] CP/M}
22         pr5 = '     trap   : boolean;';
23         pr6 = '     promax,pnindex : byte;';
24         pr7 = '{$I menu.prc}';
25         prtt = ' trap := true;';
26         prtf = ' trap := false;';
27
28
29   var includ, mode  : boolean;
30       blk       : array[0..50] of char; {40]CP/M}
31       pronam        : arstr80;
32       word          : arstr80;
33       paren         : byte;
34       bst, beg      : byte;
35       InFile        : str12;
36       lword, line   : str80;
37       source        : text;
38       inclsource    : text;
39       target        : text;
```

```
40          maxind        : byte;
41          lnumber       : integer;
42          wait, wrend   : boolean;
43          lnum          : str12;
44          tr            : char;
45          promem        : array[1..50] of
                              string[40]; {[..40] CP/M}
46          proczl        : byte;
47
48
49    function open_r (var a : text; var dt ):
                              boolean;
50
51     var d : string[12];
52
53    begin
54      move(dt, d, mem[seg(dt):ofs(dt)] + 1);
55        { move(dt, d, mem[addr(dt)] + 1);CP/M only}
56      {$i-}
57      assign(a, d);
58      reset(a);
59      if IOresult <> 0 then
60        begin
61          close(a);
63        end
64      else
65        open_r := true;
66      {$I+}
67    end;
68
69    procedure open_w (var q : text; var dn);
70    var ln, ps : byte;
71        d          : string[20];
72    begin
73      move(dn, d, 12);
74      ln := length(d);
75      ps := pos('.', d);
76      if (ps = 0) or (ps > 8) then
77        ps := 9;
78
79      delete(d, ps, ln - ps + 1);
80      d := d + '.trc';
81      assign(q, d);
82      writeln('Will create file: ',d);
```

```
83        rewrite(q);
84
85   end;
86
87   procedure field_in (zw:str80;
                            var ww:arstr80;
                            var max : byte);
88
89   const special: trz = ['{','}','(',')','*',
90                         '''',';', ':','='];
91        alfa : trz = ['a'..'z','A'..'Z','^','$'];
92        digalf:trz = ['a'..'z','A'..'Z','0'..'9',
93                      '^','$','_'];
94   var pw : byte;
95
96   begin
97     pw := 1;
98     max := 0;
99     while pw <= length(zw) do
100       begin
101         max := succ(max);
102         ww[max] := '';
103         if not (zw[pw] in alfa) then
104           begin
105             if not (zw[pw] in special) then
106               begin
107                 repeat
108                   ww[max] := ww[max] + zw[pw];
109                   pw := succ(pw);
110                 until (zw[pw] in (alfa +
                                 special)) or
111                       (pw > length(zw))
112               end
113             else
114               begin
115                 ww[max] := zw[pw];
116                 pw := succ(pw);
117                 if ((ww[max]='(') and
                         (zw[pw]='*')) or
118                    ((ww[max]='*') and
                         (zw[pw] = ')')) then
119                   begin
120                     ww[max] := ww[max] + zw[pw];
121                     pw := succ(pw);
```

```
122                      end;
123                  end;
124            end
125         else
126            begin
127               repeat
128                  ww[max]  := ww[max] + zw[pw];
129                  pw := succ(pw);
130               until  (pw > length(zw)) or not
131                      ((zw[pw] in digalf) or
132                      ((zw[pw] = '.') and
133                      (zw[pw + 1] in digalf)));
134            end;
135      end;
136 end;
137
138
139 function status(ws:arstr80; ss:byte):boolean;
140 begin
141    if not mode then
142       begin
143       if (ws[ss] = '''') and (paren = 0) then
144          mode := not mode
145       else
146          begin
147             if (ws[ss]='{')or (ws[ss]='(*') then
148                begin
149                   ss := ss + 1;
150                   if(ws[ss]='$I') or
                      (ws[ss]='$i') then
151                      begin
152                         ss := ss + 1;
153                         if not (ws[ss][1] in
                              ['+', '-']) then
154                            begin
155                               InFile := ws[ss + 1];
156                               includ := true;
157                            end
158                         else
159                            paren := paren + 1;
160                      end
161                   else
162                      paren := paren + 1;
163                end
```

```
164              else
165                if ((ws[ss]'}') or
                       (ws[ss] = '*)')) and
166                  not includ then
167                  paren := paren - 1;
168          end
169      end
170      else
171       if ws[ss] = '''' then
172         mode := not mode;
173
174      status := not (mode or includ or
                         (paren > 0));
175    end;
176
177    function vlevel(var wv:arstr80;
                             sl:byte) : boolean;
178    var     l1, l2 : byte;
179    function searchblock (st : str80) : boolean;
180
181    begin
182       searchblock := (st = 'procedure') or
183                      (st = 'program')   or
184                      (st = 'function')  or
185                      (st = 'begin')     or
186                      (st = 'case')      or
187                      (st = 'end');
188    end;
189
190    begin
191      if searchblock(wv[sl]) then
192        case wv[sl][1] of
193         'p', 'f' : begin
194                      proczl := proczl + 1;
195                      bst := bst + 1;
196                      pronam[bst] := wv[sl]+' '+
                                       wv[sl + 2];
197                      promem[proczl]:=pronam[bst];
198                    end;
199         'b' :      begin
200                      beg := succ(beg);
201                      blk[beg] := 'b';
202                      if beg = 1 then
203                        begin
```

```
204                            if bst = 1 then
205                                begin
206             writeln(target, 'begin');
207             for ll=1 to proczl do
208                                begin
209       writeln(target, 'promem[', ll, ']:=', '''',
210                       promem[ll], '''', ';');
211       writeln(target, 'prozlr[', ll, ']:=',
                             '0;');
212                                end;
213             writeln(target, 'promax:=',
214                       proczl, ';');
215             writeln(target, 'pnindex:=',
216                         '0;');
217                               if UpCase(tr) = 'Y'
                                     then
218                                  wv[sl] := prtt
219                               else
220                                  wv[sl] := prtf;
221                            end;
222                           wv[sl] := wv[sl] + al +
                                  pronam[bst] + zl;
223                        end;
224                      end;
225       'c' :        if beg > 0 then
226                        begin
227                          beg := succ(beg);
228                          blk[beg] := 'c';
229                        end;
230       'e' :        if beg > 0 then
231                        begin
232                          beg := pred(beg);
233                          if (beg = 0) and
                                (blk[1] = 'b') then
234                              begin
235                                bst := pred(bst);
236                                wv[sl] := a2+'       ' +
                                        z2 + wv[sl];
237                              end;
238                        end
239                      else if wv[sl]='external'then
240                          bst := pred(bst);
241         end;
242      vlevel := beg > 0;
```

```
243   end;
244
245   procedure insstr (var wi:arstr80; pi:byte);
246
247   var akteintr : string[80];
248
249   const  a:      trz=['a'..'z','A'..'Z',';','('];
250
251   function searchloop (a : str80) : boolean;
252   begin
253     searchloop := (a = 'begin') or
254                   (a = 'while') or
255                   (a = 'if') or
256                   (a = 'repeat') or
257                   (a = 'for');
258   end;
259
260   begin
261     akteintr := a3 + lnum + z3;
262
263     if wait then
264       begin
265         if wi[pi][1] in a then
266           begin
267             wait := false;
268             lword := wi[pi];
269             if not searchloop(wi[pi]) then
270               begin
271                 wi[pi] := 'begin ' + wi[pi];
272                 wrend := true;
273               end
274           end;
275       end
276     else
277       if   (wi[pi]='then') or (wi[pi]='do') or
278          ((blk[beg]='c') and (wi[pi =':') and
279          (wi[pi + 1] <> '=')) then
280         wait := true
281       else
282         if wi[pi] = ';' then
283           begin
284             if wrend then
285               begin
286                 wi[pi] := ';'+akteintr+ 'end;';
```

```
287                           wrend := false;
288                       end
289                   else
290                     if lword <> 'end' then
291                       wi[pi] := ';' + akteintr + ';';
292                       lword := ';';
293               end
294           else
295             if wi[pi] = 'else' then
296               begin
297                 wait := true;
298                 if wrend then
299                   begin
300                     wi[pi] := ';' + akteintr +
                                  'end ' + wi[pi];
301                     wrend := false;
302                   end
303               end
304           else
305             if ((wi[pi] = 'end') or
                    (wi[pi] = 'until')) and
306                 (lword <> 'end') and
                    (lword <>  ';') then
307               begin
308                 lword := wi[pi];
309                 wi[pi] := ';'+akteintr+ wi[pi];
310               end
311           else
312             if wi[pi][1] in a then
313               lword := wi[pi];
314   end;
315
316   procedure field_out (wo:arstr80; max:byte);
317   var po : byte;
318
319   const p:trz =['a'..'z','A'..'Z',':',',',';'];
320
321   begin
322     po := 1;
323     while po <= max do
324       begin
325         if status(wo, po) then
326           begin
327             if vlevel(wo, po) then
```

```
328                    insstr(wo, po)
329             end;
330          if not includ then
331             write(target, wo[po]);
332             po := succ(po);
333          end;
334     writeln(target);
335     writeln;
336  end;
337
338  procedure prog (var src : text);
339  var lf : byte;
340
341  begin
342     InFile := '';
343     while not eof(src) do
344        begin
345           line := '';
346           readln(src, line);
347           lnumber := lnumber + 1;
348           str(lnumber, lnum);
349
350           field_in(line, word, maxind);
351
352           gotoxy(12, 7);
353           writeln(lnum);
354
355           field_out(word, maxind);
356
357           if includ then
358              begin
359                 includ := false;
360                 if open_r(inclsource, InFile) then
361                    prog(inclsource)
362                 else
363                    close(inclsource);
364              end
365        end;
366
367     close(src);
368  end;
369
370
371
```

```
372
373    procedure init;
374
375    var ll : byte;
376
377    begin
378      repeat
379        clrscr;
380        write('File : ');
381        readln(InFile);
382      until open_r(source, InFile);
383
384      writeln;
385      write('Single step mode (y/n) : ');
386      buflen := 1;
387      readln(tr);
388      writeln;
389
390      open_w(target, InFile);
391      writeln;
392      writeln('Converting : ');
393
394      wait := false;
395      wrend := false;
396      bst := 0;
397      proczl := 0;
398      beg := 0;
399      paren := 0;
400      mode := false;
401      includ := false;
402      lnumber := 1;
403
404      line := '';
405      readln(source, line);
406      lnumber := lnumber + 1;
407      str(lnumber, lnum);
408
409      field_in(line, word, maxind);
410
411      field_out(word, maxind);
412      writeln(target, pr1);
413      writeln(target, pr2);
414      writeln(target, pr3);
415      writeln(target, pr4);
```

```
416     writeln(target, pr5);
417     writeln(target, pr6);
418     writeln(target, pr7);
419
420     end;
421
422 begin
423    init;
424    prog(source);
425    close(target);
426 end.
```

The following procedure is required by the program being converted and should be saved on your disk with the name `menu.prc`.

Menu procedure - required in your source program for convert

Save to disk under the name **menu.prc**

```
 1 procedure menu (md : byte; wd : aaaa80);
 2
 3  var   x, y : byte;
 4        l, ll, cod,
 5        zlns : integer;
 6
 7  procedure incr (w : aaaa80);
 8  var  l : integer;
 9         g : boolean;
10
11 begin
12    l := 1;
13    g := false;
14    while (l < promax) and not g do
15      begin
16        l := l + 1;
17        g := (w = promem[l]);
18      end;
19    if g then
20      prozlr[l] := prozlr[l] + 1;
21 end;
22
23 procedure wait;
24
25 var l        : integer;
26     x, y     : byte;
27     cm       : char;
28     ln, ps   : byte;
29 begin
30
31    gotoxy(40, 1);
32
33    write('Command : ');
34    read(kbd, cm);
```

```
35
36    case UpCase(cm) of
37
38     'T' : begin
39             write('T');
40             trap := not trap;
41           end;
42     'L' : begin
43             write('L');
44             for l := 2 to promax do
45               begin
46                 gotoxy(1, 1);
47                 write(promem[l], '             ');
48                 gotoxy(30, 1);
49                 write(prozlr[l]:0:0,'        ');
50                 read(kbd, cm);
51               end;
52           end;
53     'D' : begin
54             write('D');
55             ln := length(promem[1]);
56             ps := pos(' ', promem[1]);
57             ln := ln - ps + 1;
58             writeln(lst, 'Program   :  ',
                        copy(promem[1], ps, ln));
59             writeln(lst);
60             write(lst, 'Procedure/function');
61             write(lst, '                 ');
62             writeln(lst, 'Number of passes');
63             for ln := 1 to 80 do
64               write(lst, '_');
65             writeln(lst);
66             writeln(lst);
67
68             for l := 2 to promax do
69               begin
70                 write(lst, promem[l]);
71                 for ln:=1 to
                          30-length(promem[l]) do
72                   write(lst, ' ');
73                 writeln(lst,'     ',
                          prozlr[l]:8:0);
74                 writeln(lst);
75               end;
```

```
76            end;
77      end;
78
79 end;
80
81 begin {MS-DOS only} x:=WhereX; y:=WhereY;
82    case md of
83
84    1 : begin
85            gotoxy(1, 1);
86            pnindex := pnindex + 1;
87            pronam[pnindex] := wd;
88            if pnindex > 1 then
89               incr(wd);
90            write(wd, '              ');
91          end;
92    2 : if pnindex > 1 then
93          begin
94             gotoxy(1, 1);
95             pnindex := pnindex - 1;
96             wd := pronam[pnindex];
97             write(wd, '              ');
98          end;
99    3 : begin
100           gotoxy(1, 3);
101           val(wd, zlns, cod);
102           write('line : ', zlns, '     ');
103         end;
104   end;
105
106
107   if trap then
108      wait
109   else
110      if keypressed then
111         wait
112   else
113      begin
114        for l := 1 to 2000 do
115           if keypressed then
116              wait;
117      end;
118   GotoXY(x,y); {CP/M replace with - writeln;}
119   end;
```

If you are using an MS-DOS computer, you can make the following changes to the program to improve the screen output of the trace information:

After line 81 the following instructions must be added to the program:

```
x := WhereX;
y := WhereY;
```

The instruction

```
GotoXY(x,y);
```

then follows in line 118 instead of the `writeln` statement.

Appendices

Matis/T - a software tool for Turbo programmers

Pascal is a powerful and elegantly structured language, and Turbo is one of its strongest implementations. However, in order to produce an attractive and reliable user interface, and take full advantage of the sophisticated display capabilities of MS-DOS computers, the programmer must write a great deal of screen management code, often combining operating system calls and assembly language routines with the primitives of the Pascal language.

While this task may be inherently interesting to some programmers, it is also one of the most time consuming, difficult and distracting aspects of programming.

The programming tool, **Matis/T**, provides an ideal alternative. It is an integrated, versatile and powerful screen management system. Yet it is easily learned and incorporated into application programs. It consists of a logical, uniform, and well documented set of commands which greatly extend the screen input/output capabilities of Turbo Pascal.

Matis/T provides an advanced windowing capability that goes far beyond the type of window supported by Turbo Pascal. In Turbo Pascal, a window is simply a segment of the screen into which all output is confined. The Matis/T windowing system consists of two distinct elements, a *page* and a *window*. A page may contain up to 65,534 rows and 65,534 columns of constant data and input/output fields. Multiple pages may be created, limited only by available memory.

A window is a segment of the screen through which a page may be viewed. Multiple windows may be defined, and if the page is larger than the window, the page will scroll behind the window. This arrangement is ideal for laying out large input forms such as invoices or tax forms, which need not be broken up to fit on the screen, but yet may be viewed in their entirety through a single window.

When a page is displayed through a window, data may be input by the user or output from the program through any predefined fields, simply by specifying the field number in a single function call. All information about the display attributes, data type and length of a field is stored in the page and need not be specified each time the program uses the field. When data is being input to a field, **Matis/T** automatically provides basic editing functions, so that the user may backspace, delete, insert, go to the end of the field, or go to the previous field.

You can also program specific keys to interrupt data input, to supply a default values, or to display a help screen, for example. In addition, Matis/T performs preliminary validation of data as it is entered, according to your specifications.

A page may be sent directly to the printer, eliminating the need for separate operations to produce printed output. So a single page definition replaces screen formatting, attribute setting, editing functions, cursor movement commands, validation and printer formatting.

You can create a page with **Matis/T** in two ways. The first method is to use **Matis** commands in your program to build a page in memory. The second method is to use the utility *Matpage*, to interactively design a page, see the actual page layout as it is created, and even simulate data input. The page may then be saved on disk and later used by any program.

In addition to its advanced windowing capability, **Matis/T** also provides direct access to some of the unique hardware features of MS-DOS machines. All monochrome display attributes, such as reverse video, underlining, intensity and blinking, may be assigned to any element in a page. On color displays, all attributes supported by the color text mode may be used. The function and arrow keys may be defined for special purposes. Also, a number of the extended ASCII graphics characters are generated automatically through simple commands, in order to produce lines and borders to define areas of a page.

While using many specialized capabilities, **Matis/T** remains quite portable among MS-DOS machines. Matis is also available with interfaces for other important languages, such as BASIC, C, MS-Pascal, and Assembler, all of which use a common, portable set of commands.

Programmers who have used **Matis/T** have found it not only powerful and flexible, but also reliable, easily maintained, and well supported. They have commented that it has greatly increased their productivity, while enhancing their programs both visually and functionally.

Matis/T is an outstanding exemplification of the new generation of software which combines low cost with surpassing capabilities.

You may order **Matis/T** for $29.95 plus $5.00 UPS shipping and handling (Calif. res. add sales tax) from **Softway**, Inc. 500 Sutter Street, Suite 222, Dept A1, San Francisco, CA 94102 or call (415) 397-4666.

Bibliography

Date, C.J., *Database - A Primer*, Addison-Wesley, Reading, MA., 1983

Horowitz, E. and Sahni, S., *Fundamentals of Data Structures*, Computer Science Press, Potomac, MD., 1976

Jensen, K and Wirth, N., *Pascal User Manual and Report*, Springer-Verlag, New York, 1974.

Knuth, Donald., *Sorting and Searching*, Addison-Wesley, Reading, MA., 1973

Martin, J., *Computer Data-Base Organization*, Prentice-Hall, Englewood Cliffs, N.J., 1975.

Norton, P., *Programmer's Guide to the IBM PC*, Microsoft Press, Bellevue, WA, 1985.

Norton, P., *Inside the IBM PC*, Robert J. Brady, Co., Bowie, MD., 1983.

Wirth, N., *Algorithms + Data Structures = Programs*, Prentice-Hall, Englewood Cliffs, N.J., 1976.

Optional Diskette

Turbo Pascal Tricks & Tips
Optional diskette

For your convenience, the program listings contained in this book are available on either an IBM/PC formatted diskette (320K or 360K, for MS-DOS versions of the programs) or on Kaypro formatted diskette (for CP/M versions of the programs).

You should order the diskette if you want to use the programs without typing them in from the listings in the book.

All programs on the diskette have been fully tested. You can change the programs for your particular needs. The diskette is available for $14.95 + $2.00 ($5.00 foreign) for postage and handling.

When ordering, please specify the title of the diskette, the format (MS-DOS or CP/M), your name and shipping address. Enclose a check, money order or credit card information. Mail your order to:

Abacus Software
P.O. Box 7219
Grand Rapids, MI 49510

Or for fast phone service, call **616/241-5510**.

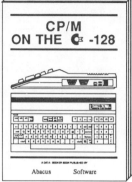

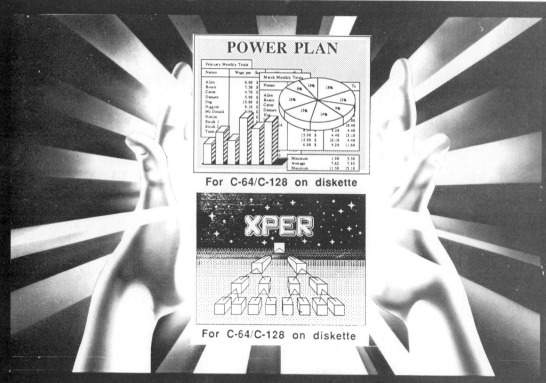

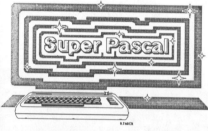
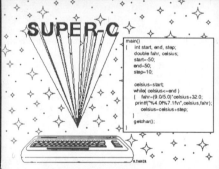

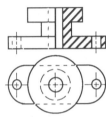
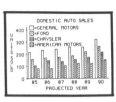
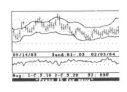

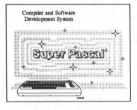
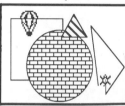

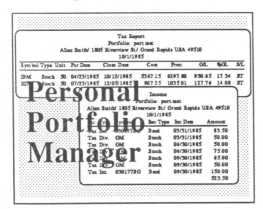
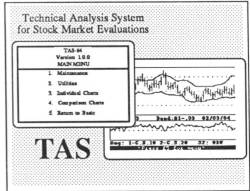